GUY·KNITS
the Best of Knitter's

a publication of  BOOKS

PUBLISHER
Alexis Yiorgos Xenakis

COEDITORS
Rick Mondragon
Elaine Rowley

EDITORIAL ASSISTANTS
Sue Kay Nelson
Elisabeth Robinson

INSTRUCTION EDITOR
Joni Coniglio

INSTRUCTION ASSISTANTS
Jill Aurand
Mary Lou Eastman
Tara Pageler
Kelly Rokke
Carol Thompson

GRAPHIC DESIGNER
Bob Natz

PHOTOGRAPHER
Alexis Xenakis

CHEIF EXECUTIVE OFFICER
Benjamin Levisay

DIRECTOR, PUBLISHING SERVICES
David Xenakis

STYLISTS
Lisa Mannes
Rick Mondragon

TECHNICAL ILLUSTRATOR
Carol Skallerud

PRODUCTION DIRECTOR & COLOR SPECIALIST
Dennis Pearson

BOOK PRODUCTION MANAGER
Greg Hoogeveen

DIGITAL PREPRESS
Everett Baker

MIS
Jason Bittner

FIRST PUBLISHED IN THE USA IN 2008 BY XRX, INC.

ISBN 13: 9781933064093
Produced in Sioux Falls, South Dakota, by XRX, Inc.,
PO Box 965, Sioux Falls, SD 57101-0965 USA 605.338.2450

a publication of XRX BOOKS

visit us online knittinguniverse.com XRX

GUY·KNITS

photography by
Alexis Xenakis

Contents

welcome

Men who knit are still in the minority, but guys love knits—let's not neglect them.

When we knit for a guy, it usually means that the knitter is not the wearer. So we need to understand what the guy is comfortable wearing. Do this, and you needn't worry about that old boyfriend-sweater curse.

As always, knit with love, but make sure that love is not blind. After all, handknits should enhance, not complicate, a relationship.

Accessories

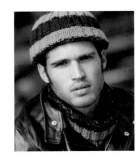

Knitter's Design Team

Cold winter commutes require warm accessories. This dickey is as warm as a scarf but without the cumbersome tails—perfect for subway, motorbike, or foot travelers. It begins at the neck and grows around the shoulders with four mitered gussets. Create another tube and decrease it into a watch cap. For a non-striped set complete with matching gauntlets, turn the page.

Warm & Ready

EASY +

One Size

DICKEY
Neck circumference 20¾"
Length 10"

HAT
Circumference 20¾"
Depth 8¼"

10cm/4"

23
17

• over k2, p2 rib

1 2 3 4 **5** 6

• **Bulky weight**
A, B, C and D • 80 yds each

• 5.5mm/US 9, 40cm (16") long,
or size to obtain gauge

HAT only • Four 5.5mm/US 9

&

stitch markers

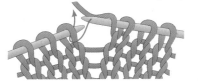

original yarn

Fairmount Fibers-MANOS DEL URUGUAY
Kettle Dyed Pure Wool (wool; 100g; 138 yds)
Goldenrod (A), Stellar (B), Mallard (C) and
Coffee (D)

Notes
1 See *School*, page 82 for SSK. **2** Dickey is worked from the top down. **3** For hat, change to dpns when necessary.

Stripe Pattern
* Work 7 rounds each with A, B, C, D; repeat from * for Stripe Pattern.

DICKEY
With circular needle and A, cast on 88 stitches (counts as round 1 of Stripe Pattern). Place marker (pm), join, and continue in Stripe Pattern as follows: work in k2, p2 rib for 27 rounds more. Piece measures approximately 5" from beginning. *Begin Dickey Gusset Chart: Round 1* Rib 20 stitches, pm, k1, RYO, k1, pm, rib 18 stitches, pm, k1, RYO, k1, pm, rib 22 stitches, pm, k1, RYO, k1, pm, rib 18 stitches, pm, k1, RYO, k1, pm, p2—92 stitches. Continue to work chart pattern between markers and all other stitches in rib pattern as established through chart round 28—196 stitches. With D, bind off.

HAT
With circular needle and A, cast on 88 stitches (counts as round 1 of Stripe Pattern). Pm, join, and continue in Stripe Pattern as follows: work in k2, p2 rib for 31 rounds more. Piece measures approximately 5½" from beginning.
Shape crown
Round 1 [K2, p2, k1, SSK, p1] 11 times. *Rounds 2 and 3* [K2, p2, k2, p1] 11 times. Cut A and continue with B to end. *Round 4* [K1, SSK, p1, k2, p1] 11 times. *Rounds 5 and 6* [K2, p1] 22 times. *Round 7* [K2, p1, k1, SSK] 11 times. *Rounds 8 and 9* [K2, p1, k2] 11 times. *Round 10* [K2, p1, SSK] 11 times. *Round 11* [K2, p1, k1] 11 times. *Round 12* [SSK, p1, k1] 11 times. *Round 13* [K1, p1, k1] 11 times. *Round 14* [SSK, k1] 11 times. *Round 15* [SSK] 11 times. Cut yarn, draw through remaining 11 stitches tightly and fasten off.

Finishing
Block pieces.

Dickey Gusset Chart

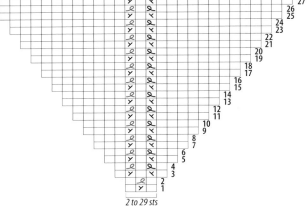

2 to 29 sts

Stitch key
☐ Knit
Right-slanting yo (RYO)
Left-slanting yo (LYO)
Knit through front loop of RYO
Knit through back loop of LYO

RIGHT-SLANTING YARN OVER (RYO)

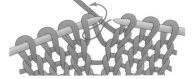

1 Bring yarn from back to front over needle, then to back again under needle. Knit next stitch on left needle.

2 On following round, knit into the front loop of the yo to twist it.

3 The result is a right-slanting increase.

LEFT SLANTING-YARN OVER (LYO)

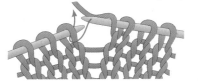

1 Bring yarn under needle to the front, take it over the needle to the back. Knit next stitch on left needle.

2 On following round, knit into the back loop of the yo to twist it.

3 The result is a left-slanting increase.

Non-Striped Set

Notes

1 See page 4 for gauge, yarn weight, and suggested needle size.

2 See *School*, page 82, for Make 1 purl (M1P).

Dickey and Hat

Work as for Striped Dickey and Hat on page 4 EXCEPT work in one color.

Gauntlets MAKE 2

Cast on 36 stitches divided over 4 dpns. Join, and work in k2, p2 rib for 30 rounds. *Begin Thumb Gusset Chart: Round 1* K2, pm, p2, M1P, k2, M1P, p2, pm, rib to end—38 stitches. Continue to work Thumb Gusset Chart between markers and all other stitches in rib pattern as established, through chart round 8—44 stitches. *Next round* K2, bind off 14 stitches in pattern, rib to end—30 stitches. *Next round* K2, pick up and knit 1 stitch in first bound-off stitch, then pick up and knit 1 stitch in last bound-off stitch, rib to end—32 stitches. Work 8 rounds in k2, p2 rib. Bind off in pattern.

Thumb Gusset Chart

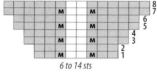

6 to 14 sts

Stitch key

☐ Knit
▨ Purl
Ⓜ M1P

UNIQUE KOLOURS-COLINETTE
Prism (merino wool, cotton; 100g; 132 yds) Pierro multi color;
3 skeins makes the set of dickey, hat, and gauntlets.

Garter stitch shaping in two colors provides a great stripe pattern for your guy. The hat is reversible and doubly thick. Add mittens and you have a look that's more fun than a snowball fight!

Susan Z. Douglas

Reversible Hat, Mittens

INTERMEDIATE

HAT - One Size
Finished Measurements
Circumference 22"

10cm/4"

36

18
• **over garter stitch (knit every row)**

1 2 3 **4** 5 6

• **Medium weight**
A • 300 yds
B & C • 200 yds each

• 4.5mm (US 7), or size to obtain gauge

• 4mm/G

&
• stitch markers

original yarn
BAABAJOES WOOL COMPANY 10-ply
(wool; 250g; 450 yds)
Goldstone (A), Brownstone (B),

Notes

1 See *School*, page 82, for SSK, Make 1 right-slanting (M1R) and left-slanting (M1L), chain cast-on, garter stitch grafting, intarsia knitting, and short rows wrap and turn (W&T). **2** When changing color, bring new color under old to prevent holes.

Wrap Stitch and Turn (W&T)
With yarn in back, slip next stitch purlwise. Pass yarn between needles to front of work, slip same stitch back to left needle. Turn work.

HAT
Chain cast on 30 stitches with A, then 68 stitches with B (counts as row 1)—98 stitches. *Row 2* (WS) K68 with B, k30 with A. Continue to knit all stitches in the following colors (working short row wraps at the same time where indicated): *Row 3* 68A, 28C, W&T. *Row 4* 28C, 66A, W&T. *Row 5* 28A, 64B, W&T. *Row 6* 64B, 26A, W&T. *Row 7* 64A, 24C, W&T. *Row 8* 24C, 62A, W&T. *Row 9* 24A, 60B, W&T. *Row 10* 60B, 22A, W&T. *Row 11* 60A, 20C, W&T. *Row 12* 20C, 58A, W&T. *Row 13* 20A, 56B, W&T. *Row 14* 56B, 18A, W&T. *Row 15* 56A, 16C, W&T. *Row 16* 16C, 54A, W&T. *Row 17* 16A, 56B, W&T. *Row 18* Repeat row 14. *Row 19* 56A, 20C, W&T. *Row 20* Repeat row 12. *Row 21* 20A, 60B, W&T. *Row 22* Repeat row 10. *Row 23* 60A, 24C, W&T. *Row 24* Repeat row 8. *Row 25* 24A, 64B, W&T. *Row 26* Repeat row 6. *Row 27* 64A, 28C, W&T. *Row 28* Repeat row 4. *Row 29* 28A, 68B. *Row 30* Repeat row 2. *Row 31* 68A, 30C. *Row 32* 30C, 68A. Repeat rows 1–32 (k30A, 68B on row 1) 4 times more, then work rows 1–31 once.

Finishing
Cut yarn, leaving tails long enough to graft open stitches to cast-on stitches. Place cast-on stitches on needle, removing chain. Graft stitches together, using garter stitch graft, and following row 32 for color. With B, gather striped end of hat by running yarn 6 times through B ridges (skipping C ridges). Pull tightly and run gathering yarn through again. Fasten off. With A, gather solid end of hat in same way.

MITTENS

Right Mitten

Cuff

With B, chain cast on 24 stitches. Work back and forth in rows as follows: Knit 1 row with B. * Knit 2 rows with C, knit 2 rows with B; repeat from * 13 (14, 15) times more. With C, knit 1 row. With C, garter stitch graft open stitches to cast-on stitches, forming a circle.

Hand

Fold cuff in half width wise, WS together, forming a doubled fabric. With RS facing and A, pick up and knit 38 (40, 42) stitches evenly around cuff, going through both layers and making sure stripes are lined up. Divide stitches over 3 double-pointed needles (dpn). Place marker (pm), join, and work 4 (6, 6) rounds in stockinette stitch.

Thumb gusset

Round 1 K21 (22, 23), pm, M1L, k1, M1R, pm, k16 (17, 18). **Round 2** Knit. **Round 3** Knit to marker, slip marker (sm), M1L, knit to marker, M1R, sm, knit to end of round. **Round 4** Knit. Repeat rounds 3–4 four times more—13 stitches between markers.

Divide for thumb and top of hand

Next round K21 (22, 23), remove marker (rm), cast on 1 stitch, place 13 thumb gusset stitches on hold, rm, k16 (17, 18)—38 (40, 42) stitches. Work 2½ (3, 3½)" in stockinette stitch.

Shape top

Decrease round [SSK, k15 (16, 17), k2tog] twice. **Next round** Knit. Repeat last 2 rounds 6 (7, 7) times more, working 2 fewer knit stitches between SSK and k2tog on each decrease round. Cut yarn, draw through remaining 10 (8, 10) stitches, pull together tightly and secure to WS.

Thumb

Divide 13 thumb stitches between 2 dpns. Join A and work as follows: **Round 1** Pick up and knit 3 stitches along inside edge of thumb, then k13—16 stitches. Work in stockinette stitch until thumb measures 1¾ (2, 2¼)". **Next round** [K2tog] 8 times. Finish as for top of mitten.

Left Mitten

Work as for right mitten, reversing thumb placement as follows:

Thumb gusset

Round 1 K16 (17, 18), pm, M1L, k1, M1R, pm, k21 (22, 23).

Divide for thumb and top of hand

Next round K16 (17, 18), cast on 1 stitch, place 13 thumb gusset stitches on hold, k21 (22, 23).

INTERMEDIATE

MITTENS S (M, L)

Finished Measurements
Circumference 7¼ (7½, 8)"

10cm/4"

29

21

• over stockinette stitch (knit every round)

Four 4mm/US 6, or size to obtain gauge

• 4mm/G

&

• stitch markers

original yarn

See hat—enough for both projects

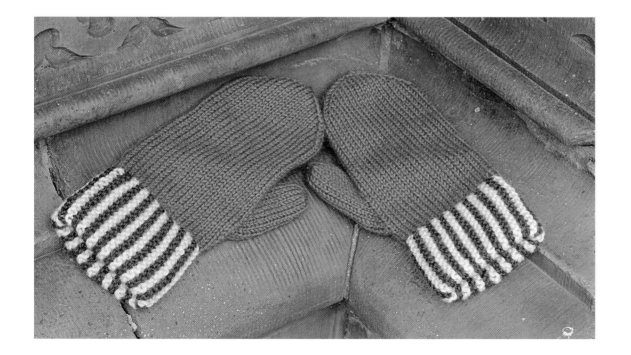

it's easy ...go for it!

EASY +

One size
46" wide x 56½" long

10cm/4"

24

15
• over Chart Pattern

1 2 3 **4** 5 6

• **Medium weight**
MC • 845 yds

1 2 3 4 **5** 6

• **Bulky weight**
A • 225 yds
B • 200 yds
C • 215 yds
D • 175 yds

• 5.5mm/US 9,
or size to obtain gauge

original yarn

LION BRAND Wool Ease (acrylic, wool; 85g;
197 yds) Chocolate (MC)
Lion Suede (polyester; 85g; 122 yds) Spice
(A), Ecru (B), Ebony (C), Mocha (D)

*Here is an afghan with boardroom style. The warm neutrals are contemporary.
The slip-stitch stripes are easy to knit in strips and become blocks when
you piece them together.*

Chaco Stripes

Notes
1 Afghan is made up of 5 panels (with 340 rows in each panel) which are knit
separately, following Chart Pattern, then sewn together. **2** When working Chart
Pattern, alternate CC between colors A, B, C, and D. Diagram shows how many rows
of each color to use for each color block of a panel. **3** For each panel, cast on the
number of stitches indicated at the bottom of the diagram, using MC, then work in
Chart Pattern, changing CC when indicated. When each panel is complete, bind off
stitches using MC.

Afghan
With MC, cast on 27 stitches for Panel 1. Work in Chart Pattern for 340 rows,
following diagram for CC changes. Work Panels 2, 3, 4 and 5.

Finishing
Block pieces. Join panels, following diagram for position of each panel.

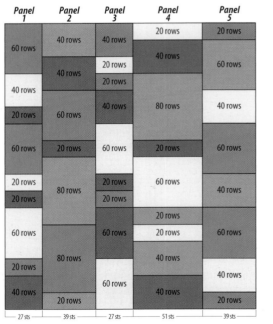

Color key
A
B
C
D

Chart Pattern

4-st repeat

Color key
☐ MC
☐ CC

Stitch key
☐ Knit on RS, purl on WS
− Purl on RS, knit on WS
∨ Slip 1 purlwise with yarn in back

Small projects give a knitter the opportunity to learn a new technique without having to commit to a long-term project. Here you'll learn to use slip stitches and sliding rows to create fabrics with two "right sides." These ties are easy to finish (they need no lining) and so practical: spill a little lunch? Just reverse your tie, and no one will know!

Heather Lodinsky

Reversibili-Ties

INTERMEDIATE+

One Size
Length approximately 55"
Width approximately 3"

7.5cm/3"

24 (38,39)

• **over pattern 1 (2, 3)**

 2 3 4 5 6

• **Super fine weight**
A & B • 110 yds each

⚒

• Two 2.5mm/US 1, or size to obtain gauge

🧵

original yarn

ROWAN Donegal Lambswool (wool; 25g; 110 yds)
1 Reversible Roll-Over Mulberry or Nutmeg (A) and Brown or Navy (B)
2 Pyramid Pattern Rose or Slate blue (A) and Black or Navy (B)
3 Colonel's Pattern Leaf green or Nutmeg (A) and Maroon or Teal (B)

Notes

1 See *School*, page 82, for long-tail cast-on. **2** Use long-tail cast-on for all ties. **3** Slip (sl) stitches purlwise with yarn in back (wyib) or with yarn in front (wyif), as indicated.

1 Reversible roll-over pattern tie

With B, cast on 24 stitches. Do not turn. Slide stitches to other end of needle.
Begin pattern: Row 1 With A, knit. Turn work. *Row 2* With B, knit. Do not turn. Slide. *Row 3* With A, purl. Turn. *Row 4* With B, purl. Do not turn. Slide. Repeat Rows 1–4 until piece measures 10" from beginning. Continue in pattern as established, decreasing 1 stitch each side every 2" 6 times—12 stitches. Work even until piece measures 55" from beginning. Bind off.

Finishing

Block.

2 Pyramid pattern tie

With A, cast on 38 stitches. Do not turn. Slide stitches to other end of needle.
Begin pattern: Row 1 With B, p1, [(k1, p1) 5 times, sl 1 wyib, sl 1 wyif] 3 times, k1. Turn work. *Row 2* With B, p1, [sl 1 wyib, sl 1 wyif, (k1, p1) 5 times] 3 times, k1. Do not turn. Slide. *Row 3* With A, p1, [(k1, p1) twice, (sl 1 wyib, sl 1 wyif) 3 times, k1, p1] 3 times, k1. Turn. *Row 4* With B, p1, [sl 1 wyib, sl 1 wyif, (k1, p1) 3 times, (sl 1 wyib, sl 1 wyif) twice] 3 times, k1. Do not turn. Slide. *Row 5* With A, p1, [(k1, p1) twice, sl 1 wyib, sl 1 wyif, (k1, p1) 3 times] 3 times, k1. Turn. *Row 6* With A, * p1, k1; repeat from * to end. Do not turn. Slide. *Row 7* With B, p1, [(k1, p1) 3 times, sl 1 wyib, sl 1 wyif, (k1, p1) twice] 3 times, k1. Turn. *Row 8* With B, p1, [(k1, p1) twice, sl 1 wyib, sl 1 wyif, (k1, p1) 3 times] 3 times, k1. Do not turn. Slide. *Row 9* With A, p1, [sl 1 wyib, sl 1 wyif, (k1, p1) 3 times, (sl 1 wyib, sl 1 wyif) twice] 3 times, k1. Turn. *Row 10* With B, p1, [(k1, p1) twice, (sl 1 wyib, sl wyif) 3 times, k1, p1] 3 times, k1. Do not turn. Slide. *Row 11* With A, p1, [sl 1 wyib, sl 1 wyif, (k1, p1) 5 times] 3 times, k1. Turn. *Row 12* With A, * p1, k1; repeat from * to end. Do not turn. Slide. Repeat Rows 1–12 until piece measures 10" from beginning. Continue in pattern as established, decreasing 1 stitch each side every 1" 10 times (working decreases 1 stitch in from each edge)—18 stitches. Work even until piece measures 55" from beginning. Bind off in rib.

Finishing

Block.

3 Colonel's pattern tie

Note When both colors are at beginning of row, bring working yarn under non-working yarn (to anchor it) before starting.
P-str Purl stitch on left needle, then wyib, lift A strand from front of work onto right needle so that it rests between first and second stitches; sl first stitch on right needle to left needle, let strand fall off right needle, then replace stitch on right needle.
K-str Knit stitch on left needle, then wyif, lift A strand from back of work onto right needle so that it rests between first and second stitches; sl first stitch on right needle to left needle, let strand fall off right needle, then replace stitch on right needle
With B, cast on 39 stitches. Turn work. *Preparation row* With B, p1, * k1, p1; repeat from * to end. Do not turn. Slide stitches to other end of needle. *Row 1* With A, sl 1 wyif, k1, * sl 5 wyif, k1; repeat from *, end sl 1 wyif. Turn. *Row 2* With B, k1, sl 1 wyif, k1, * [p1, k1] twice, sl 1 wyif, k1; repeat from * to end. Turn. *Row 3* With B, p1, k1, p1, * k1, p-str, [k1, p1] twice; repeat from * to end. Turn. *Row 4* With A, sl 4 wyif, * k1, sl 5 wyif; repeat from *, end k1, sl 4 wyif. Do not turn. Slide. *Row 5* With B, k1, p1, k1, * p1, sl 1 wyib, [k1, p1] twice; repeat from * to end. Turn. *Row 6* With B, p1, k-str, p1, * [k1, p1] twice, k-str, p1; repeat from * to end. Do not turn. Slide. Repeat Rows 1–6 until piece measures 10" from beginning. Continue in pattern as established, decreasing 1 stitch each side every 1" 10 times—19 stitches. Work even until piece measures 55" from beginning. Bind off in rib.

Finishing

Block.

PYRAMID PATTERN

REVERSIBLE ROLL-OVER PATTERN

COLONEL'S PATTERN

Sweaters

Knitter's Design Team

This fairly traditional sweater was adapted for the first issue of Knitter's Magazine from Mary Wright's Cornish Guernseys and Knit-frocks (the Lattice pattern on page 31). Here we have reworked it for a quicker knit.

Guernsey Sweater

INTERMEDIATE

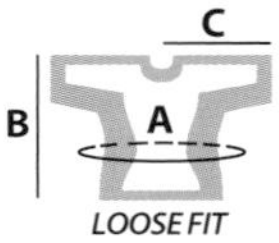

LOOSE FIT

Shown in Large
M (L, 1X, 2X)
A 44 ¼ (48, 51 ¾, 55 ¾)"
B 26 (26 ½, 28, 29)"
C 32 (33, 34, 35)"

10cm/4"

37
25
• over stockinette stitch (knit every round),
using larger needle

10cm/4"
41
25
• over Yoke Chart, using larger needles

1 **2** 3 4 5 6

• **Fine weight**
• 1800 (2000, 2200, 2400) yds

3.25mm/US 3 and 3.5mm/US 4, 40cm (16")
and 80cm (32") long, or size to obtain gauge

Five each 3.25mm/US 3 and 3.5mm/US 4

&

• stitch holders
• stitch markers

original yarn

EMU 5-ply Guernsey wool
(wool; 50g; 125 yds) Dark navy
Reknit (as shown on pages 17 and 18) DALE
Heilo (wool; 50g; 110 yds) #5563

Notes
1 See *School*, page. 82, for SSK, S2KP2, Make 1 right-slanting (M1R) and left-slanting (M1L), and 3-needle bind-off. **2** Sweater is worked circularly to underarm, then divided and front and back are worked separately back and forth in rows. Stitches for sleeves are picked up around armhole edge and sleeve is worked circularly (change to dpns when necessary). **3** Use longer or shorter circular needle, as needed. **4** Use a different-color marker for beginning of round marker.

Welt Pattern
Rounds 1 and 2 Knit. *Rounds 3 and 4* Purl. Repeat rounds 1-4 for Welt Pattern.

Seed stitch "seam" OVER 3 STITCHES
Round 1 P1, k1, p1.
Round 2 K1, p1, k1.
Repeat rounds 1 and 2 for Seed stitch "seam."

Body
With smaller needle, cast on 248 (270, 292, 314) stitches. Place marker (pm), join and work in Welt Pattern for 24 rounds. Change to larger needle. *Begin Body Pattern: Round 1* *Work Seed stitch "seam" over 3 stitches, pm, k121 (132, 143, 154) and increase 14 (15, 16, 17) stitches evenly across to get 135 (147, 159, 171) stitches*, pm; repeat from * to * once—276 (300, 324, 348) stitches. *Round 2* [Work Seed stitch "seam" over 3 stitches, knit to next marker] twice. Continue in pattern as established until piece measures 12½" from beginning, end with round 2 of Seed stitch. *Begin Lower Gusset Chart and Yoke Chart: Round 1* *Work Lower Gusset Chart over 3 stitches, work 6-stitch repeat of Yoke Chart 22

(24, 26, 28) times, then work first 3 stitches of chart once more; repeat from * once more—280 (304, 328, 352) stitches. Continue in pattern as established through round 37 of Lower Gusset Chart—328 (352, 376, 400) stitches.
Divide for front and back
Place 29 gusset stitches on holder, keeping markers in place, place next 135 (147, 159, 171) stitches on 2nd holder (for front), place next 29 gusset stitches on 3rd holder, keeping markers in place. Begin working back and forth in rows on back stitches.

Back
Next row (WS) K3 (garter stitch border), pm, then reading chart from left to right, work row 38 of Yoke Chart to last 6 stitches, work 3 chart stitches (ending at center of repeat), pm, k3 (garter stitch border). Continue in chart pattern as established, keeping 3 stitches at each edge in garter stitch (knit every row), until armhole measures 10 (10½, 12, 13)", end with a WS row. *Next row* (RS) K45 (48, 54, 58), bind off center 45 (51, 51, 55) stitches, work to end. Place stitches on hold.

Front
With WS facing, join yarn to front stitches and work as for back until armhole measures 7¼ (7¾, 9¼, 10¼)", end with a WS row.
Shape neck
Next row (RS) Work 58 (61, 67, 71) stitches, join 2nd ball of yarn and bind off center 19 (25, 25, 29) stitches, work to end. Working both sides at same time, decrease 1 stitch at each neck edge every RS row 13 times—45 (48, 54, 58) stitches each

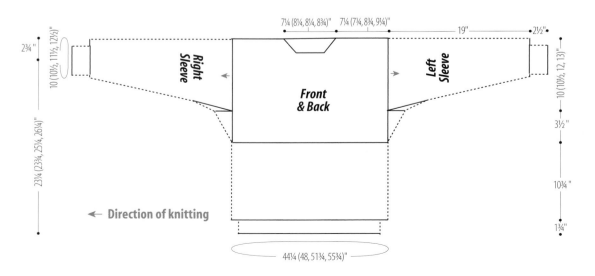

← Direction of knitting

2¾"
10 (10½, 11½, 12½)"
23¾ (23¾, 25¼, 26¼)"

7¼ (8¼, 8¼, 8¾)"   7¼ (7¾, 8¾, 9¼)"   19"   2½"

Right Sleeve   **Left Sleeve**

Front & Back

10 (10½, 12, 13)"
3½"
10¾"
1¾"

44¼ (48, 51¾, 55¾)"

side. Work even until armhole measures same length as back to shoulder. Join shoulders, using 3-needle bind-off.

Sleeves

With RS facing and larger needle, knit 29 gusset stitches from holder, then pick up and knit 123 (135, 153, 165) stitches evenly around armhole edge—152 (164, 182, 194) stitches. Join and work in rounds. *Begin Upper Gusset Chart and Yoke Chart: Round 1* Work Upper Gusset Chart over 29 stitches, work 6-stitch repeat of Yoke Chart 20 (22, 25, 27) times, then work first 3 stitches of chart once more. Continue in patterns as established through round 37 of Upper Gusset Chart—126 (138, 156, 168) stitches. *Next round* Work round 2 of Seed stitch "seam" over 3 stitches, then work pattern as established to end. *Decrease round* Work 3 stitches Seed stitch, k2tog, work to last 2 stitches, SSK. *Repeat Decrease round* every other round 0 (0, 12, 18) times, every 4th round 23 (35, 29, 26) times, every 6th round 8 (0, 0, 0) times, AT SAME TIME, when 46 rounds of Yoke Chart have been worked twice from beginning, work rounds 1-6 once more, then continue in stockinette stitch (keeping first 3 stitches of round in Seed stitch). After all decreases have been worked, there are 62 (66, 72, 78) stitches. Work even until sleeve measures 19" from pick-up round. Change to smaller needle. Knit 1 round, decreasing 6 (10, 8, 10) stitches evenly around—56 (56, 64, 68) stitches. Work in k2, p2 rib for 2½". Bind off in pattern.

Finishing

Block piece.

Neckband

With RS facing and smaller needle, begin at left shoulder and pick up and knit 22 stitches evenly along left front neck, 19 (25, 25, 29) stitches along center front neck, 22 sts along right front neck and 45 (51, 51, 55) stitches along back neck—108 (120, 120, 128) stitches. Pm, join and work in k2, p2 rib for 1". Bind off in pattern.

Upper Gusset Chart

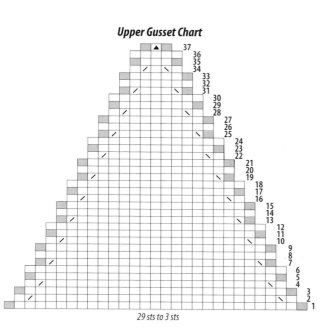

29 sts to 3 sts

Yoke Chart

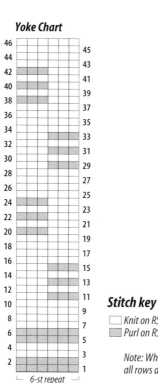

6-st repeat

Stitch key

☐ Knit on RS, purl on WS
▨ Purl on RS, knit on WS

Note: When working circularly, all rows are RS rows.

Lower Gusset Chart

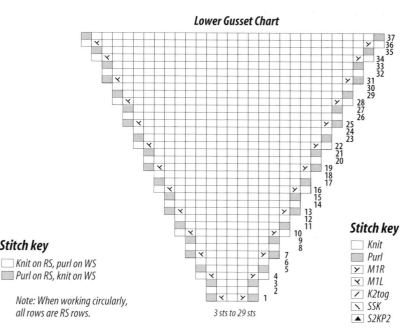

3 sts to 29 sts

Stitch key

☐ Knit
▨ Purl
⤸ M1R
⤹ M1L
╱ K2tog
╲ SSK
▲ S2KP2

Oscar Britt

A quick glance at this dramatic color pattern is apt to miss one of its best features: it's an easy, one-color-per-row, slip-stitch pattern. Make it subtle or make it bold — either way it's a fun knit.

Bold Zebra

INTERMEDIATE

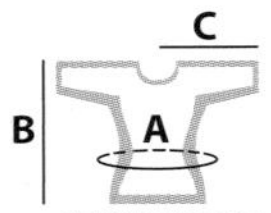

STANDARD FIT

Sizes S (M , L, 1X, 2X)
shown in Medium
A 41 (44½, 47½, 51, 54½)"
B 25½ (26, 26½, 27, 27½)"
C 32 (33, 34, 34½, 35)"

10cm/4"

37 ▦

24

• over Chart Pattern, using larger needles

1 2 3 **4** 5 6

• **Medium weight**
MC • 1000 (1050, 1175, 1250, 1350) yds
CC • 800 (850, 950, 1000, 1075) yds

4mm/US 6 and 5.5mm/US 9,
or size to obtain gauge

4mm/US 6, 40cm/16" long

&

• stitch marker

original yarn

RAINBOW MILLS Pebbles (cotton, rayon; 50g; 60yds) Black (MC) and Variegated (CC)
Reknit (as shown on pages 19 and 21): BROWN SHEEP, INC. Nature Spun Worsted Weight (wool; 100g; 245yds) Bulldog blue (MC) and NORO Silk Garden Lite (silk, mohair, wool; 50g; 137yds) #2023 (CC)

Notes

1 Keep 1 stitch at each edge in garter stitch (knit every row) for selvage. **2** You may choose to purchase extra multicolored yarn to make it easier to match colors when joining a new ball.

Back

With smaller needles and MC, cast on 103 (113, 123, 133, 143) stitches. Work in k1, p1 rib for 1¾", end with a WS row. Change to larger needles. *Next row* (RS) Knit, increasing 20 stitches evenly across—123 (133, 143, 153, 163) stitches. With CC, purl 1 row. *Begin Chart Pattern: Row 1* (RS) K1 (selvage), then beginning as indicated for back, work in Chart Pattern to last stitch, ending as indicated, k1 (selvage). Continue in pattern as established until piece measures 17½" from beginning, end with a WS row.

Shape armholes

Bind off 12 (14, 16, 18, 20) stitches at beginning of next 2 rows—99 (105, 111, 117, 123) stitches. Work even until armhole measures 8 (8½, 9, 9½, 10)". Bind off.

Front

Work as for back until armhole measures 4½ (4½, 5, 5, 5½)", end with a WS row.

Shape neck

Next row (RS) Work 43 (45, 48, 50, 53) stitches, join 2nd ball of yarn and bind off center 13 (15, 15, 17, 17) stitches, work to end. Working both sides at same time, decrease 1 stitch at each neck edge every RS row 14 (15, 15, 15, 15) times—29 (30, 33, 35, 38) stitches each side. Work even until armhole measures same length as back to shoulder. Bind off.

Sleeves

With smaller needles and MC, cast on 51 (51, 61, 61, 61) stitches. Work in k1, p1 rib for 1¾", end with a WS row. Change to larger needles. *Next row* (RS) Knit, increasing 10 stitches evenly across—61 (61, 71, 71, 71) stitches. With CC, purl 1 row. *Begin Chart Pattern: Row 1* (RS) K1, then beginning as indicated for sleeve, work in Chart Pattern to last stitch, ending as indicated, k1. Continue in pattern as established, AT SAME TIME, increase 1 stitch each side (working increases into pattern) on 9th (7th, 7th, 7th, 5th) row, then every 10th (8th, 8th, 8th, 6th) row 15 (12, 2, 17, 7) times, every 12th (10th, 10th, 10th, 8th) row 2 (8, 16, 4, 17) times—97 (103, 109, 115, 121) stitches. Piece measures approximately 21¾" from beginning. Work even for 2 (2¼, 2¾, 3, 3¼)". Bind off.

Finishing

Block pieces. Sew shoulders.

Neckband

With RS facing, circular needle and MC, begin at left shoulder and pick up and knit 25 (27, 27, 29, 29) stitches evenly along left front neck, 13 (15, 15, 17, 17) stitches along center front neck, 25 (27, 27, 29, 29) stitches along right front neck, and 41 (45, 45, 47, 47) stitches along back neck—104 (114, 114, 122, 122) stitches. Place marker, join, and work in k1, p1 rib for 1¼". Bind off in rib.
Sew top of sleeves to straight edges of armholes. Sew straight portion at top of sleeves to bound-off armhole stitches. Sew side and sleeve seams.

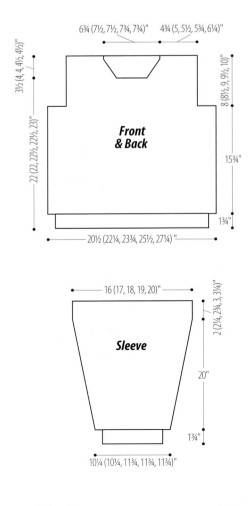

6¾ (7½, 7½, 7¾, 7¾)"   4¾ (5, 5½, 5¾, 6¼)"

3½ (4, 4, 4½, 4½)"

8 (8½, 9, 9½, 10)"

22 (22, 22½, 22½, 23)"

Front & Back

15¾"

1¾"

20½ (22¼, 23¾, 25½, 27¼)"

16 (17, 18, 19, 20)"

2 (2¼, 2¾, 3, 3¼)"

Sleeve

20"

1¾"

10¼ (10¼, 11¾, 11¾, 11¾)"

Chart Pattern

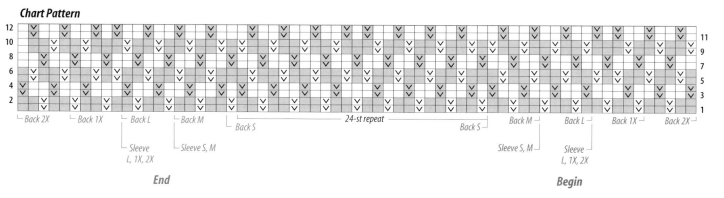

Men who love tweeds will find this a perfect option for sweater dressing. The silhouette and wide shawl collar are comfortable and warm. The rich green and split cables make a truly handsome fabric.

Kathy Zimmerman

Forks In The Road

INTERMEDIATE

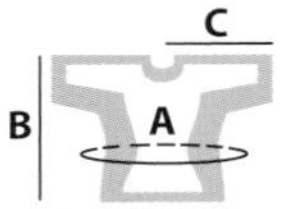

LOOSE FIT

Shown in Medium/Large
S (M/L, 1X/2X, 3X)
A 42 (48½, 55½, 62½)"
B 26 (26, 27, 27½)"
C 29 (31, 33, 35)"

10cm/4"

24

21
• over Chart Pattern, using larger needles

1 2 3 **4** 5 6

• Medium weight
• 1675 (1850, 2125, 2600) yds

• 4.5mm/US 7 and 5.5mm/US 9,
or size to obtain gauge

• 4.5mm/US 7, 60cm/24" long

&

• cable needle (cn)

original yarn

TAHKI/STACY CHARLES Donegal Tweed
(wool; 100g; 183yds) Green

Note
Keep 1 stitch at each edge in stockinette stitch (knit on RS, purl on WS) for selvage stitch.
Rib Pattern MULTIPLE OF 9 STITCHES, PLUS 2
Row 1 (WS) P4, * k3, p6; repeat from *, end k3, p4.
Row 2 K4, * p3, k6; repeat from *, end p3, k4.
Repeat Rows 1 and 2 for Rib Pattern.

Back
With smaller needles, cast on 110 (128, 146, 164) stitches. Work in Rib Pattern for 15 rows. Change to larger needles. Work in Chart Pattern until piece measures 17 (17, 17½, 17½)" from beginning, end with a WS row.
Shape armholes
Bind off 14 (18, 22, 26) stitches at beginning of next 2 rows—82 (92, 102, 112) stitches. Work even until armhole measures 9 (9, 9½, 10)". Bind off.

Front
Work as for back until armhole measures 2 (2, 2½, 3)", end with a WS row.
Shape neck
Next row (RS) Work 26 (29, 32, 35) stitches, join 2nd ball of yarn and bind off center 30 (34, 38, 42) stitches, work to end. Working both sides at same time, work even until armhole measures same length as back to shoulder. Bind off.

Sleeves
With smaller needles, cast on 56 stitches. Work in Rib Pattern for 15 rows. Change to larger needles. Work in Chart Pattern, AT SAME TIME, increase 1 stitch each side (working increase into pattern inside selvage stitches) on 3rd row, then every 4th row 8 (8, 16, 23) times, every 6th row 10 (10, 5, 1) times—94 (94, 100, 106) stitches. Piece measures approximately 18½ (18½, 19, 19½)" from beginning. Work 2¾ (3½, 4¼, 5)" even. Bind off.

Finishing
Block pieces. Sew shoulders.
Collar
With RS facing and circular needle, begin at lower right corner of neck and pick up and knit 36 (37, 38, 36) stitches evenly along right front neck, 29 (33, 37, 41) stitches along back neck, and 36 (37, 38, 36) stitches along left front neck—101 (107, 113, 113) stitches. *Begin Rib Pattern: Row 1* (WS) P1, * p3, k3; repeat from *, end p4. *Row 2* K1, *k3, p3; repeat from *, end k4. Repeat Rows 1 and 2 until collar measures 5¾ (6½, 7¼, 8)". Bind off loosely in pattern. Sew edges of collar along center front neck, overlapping left over right. Sew top of sleeves to straight edges of armholes. Sew straight portion at top of sleeves to bound-off armhole stitches. Sew side and sleeve seams.

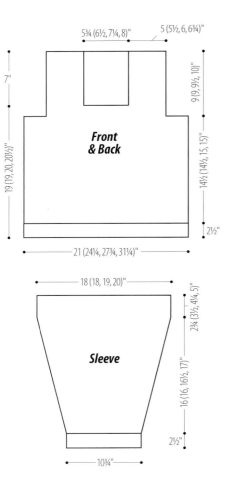

5¾ (6½, 7¼, 8)" 5 (5½, 6, 6¾)"

7"

9 (9, 9½, 10)"

19 (19, 20, 20½)"

14½ (14½, 15, 15)"

Front & Back

2½"

21 (24¼, 27¾, 31¼)"

18 (18, 19, 20)"

2¾ (3½, 4¼, 5)"

Sleeve

16 (16, 16½, 17)"

2½"

10¾"

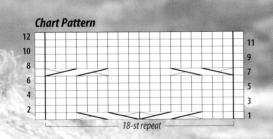

Chart Pattern

18-st repeat

Stitch key

☐ Knit on RS, purl on WS

⟋⟍ **3/3 RC** Sl 3 to cn, hold to back, k3; k3 from cn.

⟍⟋ **3/3 LC** Sl 3 to cn, hold to front, k3; k3 from cn.

Uschi Nolte

With tri-colored cables, this fun and clever design will be noticed—whether it's coming or going. Intarsia has never looked better!

Off Ramps

INTERMEDIATE

OVERSIZED FIT

Shown in Medium
S (M, L, 1X, 2X)

A 43 (46½, 50, 53½, 57)"
B 25 (25½, 26, 26½, 27)"
C 32 (33, 34, 35, 35½)"

10cm/4"

28

18

• over stockinette stitch, (knit on RS, purl on WS), using larger needles and MC

1 2 **3** 4 5 6

• **Light weight**
MC • 1325 (1430, 1560, 1670,1800) yds
CC 1 and CC 3 • 214 yds each
CC 2 • 107 (117, 127, 137, 147) yds

• 4.5mm/US 7 and 5mm/US 8, or size to obtain gauge

• 4.5mm/US 7, 40cm/16" long

&

• cable needle (cn)
• stitch markers

original yarn

JO SHARP DK Tweed (wool; 50g; 130 yds) in Brown (MC); DK Wool (wool; 50g; 107 yds) in Ruby (CC1), Chartreuse (CC2), and Blue (CC3)

Notes

1 See *School,* page 82, for intarsia. **2** Bring new color under old color at color changes to prevent holes. **3** Use a separate ball of yarn for each section of MC.

Back

With smaller needles and MC, cast on 99 (105, 111, 117, 123) stitches. Work in k1, p1 rib for 1", increasing 21 (23, 25, 27, 29) stitches evenly across last (WS) row—120 (128, 136, 144, 152) stitches. Change to larger needles. *Begin Chart Pattern: Row 1* (RS) With MC, k18 (22, 26, 30, 34), place marker (pm), work 28-stitch repeat of chart 3 times (working center 14 stitches first with CC1, then CC2, then CC3), pm, with MC, knit to end. Continue in pattern as established, working first and last 18 (22, 26, 30, 34) stitches in stockinette stitch, until piece measures 25 (25½, 26, 26½, 27)" from beginning. Bind off.

Front

Work as for back until piece measures 21½ (22, 22½, 23, 23½)" from beginning, end with a WS row.

Shape neck

Next row (RS) Work 53 (57, 60, 63, 66) stitches, bind off center 14 (14, 16, 18, 20) stitches, work to end. Working both sides at same time, bind off from each neck edge 4 stitches 0 (1, 1, 1, 1) time, 3 stitches 2 (1, 1, 1, 1) times, 2 stitches once, 1 stitch 4 times—41 (44, 47, 50, 53) stitches each side. Work even until piece measures same length as back to shoulder. Bind off.

Right Sleeve

With smaller needles and MC, cast on 41 (41, 45, 45, 45) stitches. Work in k1, p1 rib for 1", increasing 13 (13, 19, 19, 19) stitches evenly across last (WS) row—54 (54, 64, 64, 64) stitches. Change to larger needles. *Begin Chart Pattern: Row 1* (RS) With MC, k13 (13, 18, 18, 18), pm, work Chart Pattern over 28 stitches (using CC1), pm, with MC, knit to end. Continue in pattern as established, AT SAME TIME, increase 1 stitch each side (working increases into stockinette stitch with MC) every 4th row 10 (25, 10, 16, 16) times, then every 6th row 16 (6, 16, 12, 12) times—106 (116, 116, 120, 120) stitches. Work even until piece measures 21½" from beginning. Bind off.

Left Sleeve

Work as for right sleeve, except use CC3, and begin first repeat of chart with row 17.

Finishing

Block pieces. Sew shoulders.

Neckband

With RS facing, circular needle and MC, begin at left shoulder and pick up and knit 50 (52, 54, 56, 58) stitches evenly along front neck and 36 (38, 40, 42, 44) stitches along back neck—86 (90, 94, 98, 102) stitches. Pm, join, and work in k1, p1 rib for 1". Bind off.

Place markers 11 (12, 12, 12½, 12½)" down from shoulders on front and back for armholes. Sew top of sleeves between markers. Sew side and sleeve seams.

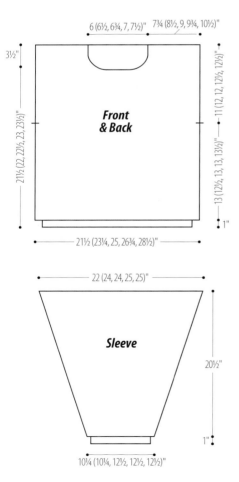

6 (6½, 6¾, 7, 7½)"   7¾ (8½, 9, 9¾, 10½)"

3½"

Front & Back

21½ (22, 22½, 23, 23½)"

11 (12, 12, 12½, 12½)"

13 (12½, 13, 13, 13½)"

1"

21½ (23¼, 25, 26¾, 28½)"

22 (24, 24, 25, 25)"

Sleeve

20½"

1"

10¼ (10¼, 12½, 12½, 12½)"

Chart Pattern

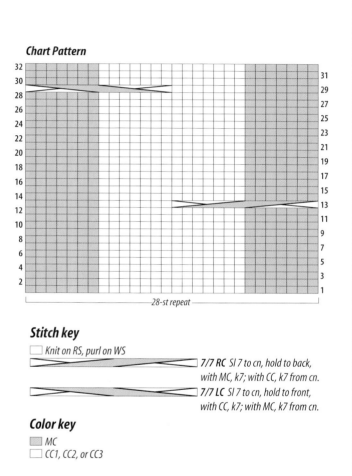

28-st repeat

Stitch key

☐ Knit on RS, purl on WS

7/7 RC Sl 7 to cn, hold to back, with MC, k7; with CC, k7 from cn.

7/7 LC Sl 7 to cn, hold to front, with CC, k7; with MC, k7 from cn.

Color key

▨ MC
☐ CC1, CC2, or CC3

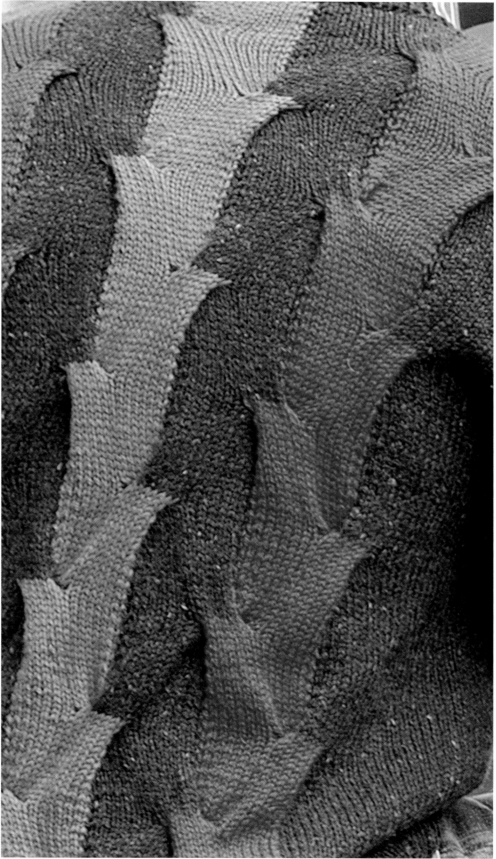

The silk-wool blend yarn is perfect for a light-weight cable sweater with Viking inspirations. The shape is simple, the cables are graphic and handsome.

Elsebeth Lavold

Hjalte

INTERMEDIATE +

C
B | A
OVERSIZED FIT

Shown in M/L
M/L (1X/2X)
A 50½ (58½)"
B 29¼"
C 35 (35½)"

10cm/4"

32

24
• over stockinette stitch (knit on RS, purl on WS), using larger needles

1 2 **3** 4 5 6

• **Light weight**
• 2220 (2400) yds

• 3.5mm/US 4 and 4mm/US 6, or size to obtain gauge

&

• cable needle (cn)
• stitch holders

original yarn

ELSEBETH LAVOLD DESIGNER'S CHOICE Silky Wool (wool, silk; 50g; 192 yds) medium gray

Note

See *School*, page 82, for SSK, Make 1 purl (M1P), lifted increase and 3-needle bind-off.

Back

With smaller needles, cast on 142 (166) stitches. *Begin Rib pattern and Chart A: Row 1* (RS) [K2, p2] 2 (5) times, * k2, work 8 stitches Chart A, [k2, p2] 7 times; repeat from * twice more, k2, work 8 stitches Chart A, [k2, p2] 2 (5) times, k2. *Row 2* [P2, k2] 2 (5) times, * p2, work 8 stitches Chart A, [p2, k2] 7 times; repeat from * twice more, p2, work 8 stitches Chart A, [p2, k2] 2 (5) times, p2. Continue in patterns as established for 28 rows more. Change to larger needles. *Increase Row* (RS) K10 (22), * work 8 stitches Chart A as established, k2, p2, M1P, p6, M1P, p10, M1P, p6, M1P, p2, k2; repeat from * twice more, work 8 stitches Chart A, k10 (22)—154 (178) stitches. *Next row* (WS) P10 (22), * work 8 stitches Chart A, p2, k30, p2; repeat from * twice more, work 8 stitches Chart A, p10 (22). *Begin Chart B: Row 1* (RS) K10 (22), * work 8 stitches Chart A, work Chart B over 34 stitches; repeat from * twice more, work 8 stitches Chart A, knit to end. Continue in patterns as established until 52 rows of Chart B have been worked twice, then work rows 1–20 (1–16) once more. Piece measures approximately 18¾ (18¼)" from beginning.

Shape armholes

Bind off 2 stitches at beginning of next 2 rows. Decrease 1 stitch each side on next row, then every other (every) row 7 (15) times more—158 (166) stitches. Work even until armhole measures approximately 9½ (10)", end with row 44 of Chart B.

Shape neck

Next row (RS) Work 60 (64) stitches, join 2nd ball of yarn and bind off center 38 stitches, work to end. Working both sides at same time, bind off from each neck edge 3 stitches once—57 (61) stitches each side. Work even through row 52 of Chart B—49 (53) stitches each side. Place stitches on hold.

Front

Work as for back until armhole measures approximately 6½ (7)", end with row 20 of Chart B.

Shape neck

Next row (RS) Work 63 (67) stitches, join 2nd ball of yarn and bind off center 32 stitches, work to end. Working both sides at same time, decrease 1 stitch at each neck edge every RS row 6 times—57 (61) stitches each side. Work even until armhole measures same length as back—49 (53) stitches each side. Place stitches on hold.

Sleeves

Cabled band

With larger needles, cast on 6 stitches. Work center 6 stitches of Chart A only until 4 rows of chart have been worked 26 (27) times. Bind off.
With RS facing and larger needles, pick up and knit 66 (70) stitches along left edge

of cabled band. Beginning with a purl row, work in stockinette stitch, AT SAME TIME, increase 1 stitch each side every 4th row 22 (25) times, then every 6th row 8 (6) times—126 (132) stitches. Work even until piece measures 18½" from beginning, end with a WS row.

Shape cap

Bind off 2 stitches at beginning of next 2 rows. Decrease 1 stitch each side on next row, then every other (every) row 7 (15) times more. Work 1 (0) row even. Bind off remaining 106 (96) stitches.

Cuff

With RS facing and smaller needles, pick up and knit 58 (62) stitches evenly along other side edge of cabled band. *Begin Rib pattern: Row 1* (WS) P2, * k2, p2; repeat from * to end. Continue in rib pattern as established until cuff measures 3". Bind off in rib.

Finishing

Join shoulders, using 3-needle bind-off.

Neckband

Work cabled band same as for sleeve until 4 rows of Chart A have been worked 47 times. Bind off.
With RS facing and smaller needles, pick up and knit 98 stitches along left edge of cabled band. Work rib pattern as for cuff for 3½". Bind off in rib.
Beginning at shoulder, sew other edge of cabled band around neck edge. Sew seam. Set in sleeves. Sew side and sleeve seams.

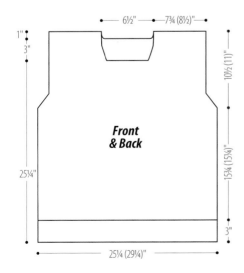

6½" — 7¾ (8½)"

1"
3"

10½ (11)"

Front & Back

25¼"

15¾ (15¼)"

3"

25¼ (29¼)"

Chart A

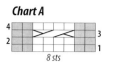

8 sts

Chart B

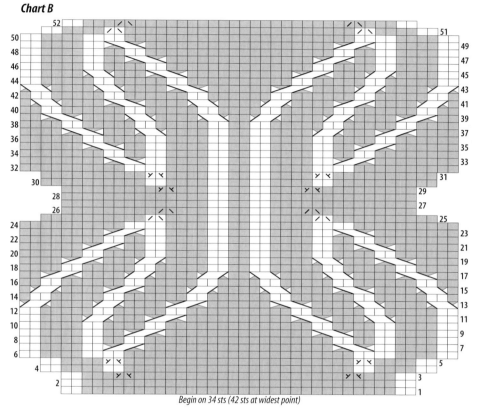

Begin on 34 sts (42 sts at widest point)

21 (22)"

Sleeve

2¼"

18"

½"

3"

11 (11½)"

← Direction of knitting

Stitch key

☐ Knit on RS, purl on WS

▨ Purl on RS, knit on WS

☑ Right knit lifted increase

☒ Left knit lifted increase

☑ Right purl lifted increase

☒ Left purl lifted increase

◺ SSK on RS

◹ K2tog on RS

◺ SSK on WS

◹ K2tog on WS

2/1 RPC Sl 1 to cn, hold to back, k2; p1 from cn.

2/1 LPC Sl 2 to cn, hold to front, p1; k2 from cn.

2/2 RC Sl 2 to cn, hold to back, k2; k2 from cn.

2/2 RPC Sl 2 to cn, hold to back, k2; p2 from cn.

2/2 LPC Sl 2 to cn, hold to front, p2; k2 from cn.

Traveling stitches form a handsome grid design in relief, and contrasting rows add a tailored edge to this deep red pullover.

Katharine Hunt

Gridlock

INTERMEDIATE

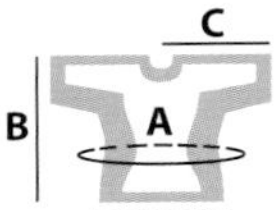

Shown in Large
S (L, 1X)
A 40 (47, 53½)"
B 24½ (27¼, 27¾)"
C 30½ (31, 32½)"

10cm/4"

27

21½
• over Chart Pattern, using larger needles

1 2 3 **4** 5 6

• **Medium weight**
MC 1600 (1900, 2200) yds
CC 50 yds for each size

• 4mm/US 6 and 5mm/US 8,
or size to obtain gauge

• 4.5mm/US 7 and 5mm/US 8,
60cm/24" long

&

• cable needle (cn)
• stitch markers

original yarn

DALE OF NORWAY Freestyle
(superwash wool; 50g; 88 yds)
in Red (MC), Charcoal (CC)

Notes

1 See *School,* page 82, for wrapping stitches on short rows. **2** Do not work 1/1 RT or 1/1 LT at edges; keep at least 1 stitch at each edge in stockinette stitch (knit on RS, purl on WS).

Back

With smaller straight needles and CC, cast on 107 (125, 143) stitches. *Begin Rib Pattern* Work in k1, p1 rib for 2 rows. Change to MC. Continue in rib pattern until ribbing measures 1½ (1½, 2)" from beginning, increase 1 stitch on last (WS) row—108 (126, 144) stitches. Change to larger needles. Work Chart Pattern, beginning and ending as indicated for back, until piece measures approximately 14½ (15¾, 16¼)" from beginning, end with chart row 16 (24, 24).

Shape armholes

Bind off 6 (8, 12) stitches at beginning of next 2 rows—96 (110, 120) stitches. Work even until armhole measures approximately 8¾ (10¼, 10¼)", end with chart row 4 (22, 22). Mark center 28 (28, 32) stitches.

Shape shoulders and neck

Bind off 7 (9, 10) stitches at beginning of next 2 (4, 6) rows, then 8 (10, 11) stitches at beginning of next 6 (4, 2) rows (for shoulders), AT SAME TIME, after 2 rows of shoulder shaping have been worked, join 2nd ball of yarn and bind off center 28 (28, 32) stitches for neck and, working both sides at same time, decrease 1 stitch at each neck edge every row 3 times.

Front

Work as for back until armhole measures approximately 3¼ (4¾, 4¾)", end with chart row 2 (20, 20).

Shape V-neck

Next row (RS) Work 47 (54, 59) stitches, join 2nd ball of yarn and bind off center 2 stitches, work to end. Working both sides at same time, decrease 1 stitch at each neck edge every other row 12 (12, 16) times, then every 4th row 4 (4, 2) times, AT SAME TIME, when piece measures same length as back to shoulders, shape shoulders as for back.

Sleeves

With smaller straight needles and CC, cast on 53 (57, 61) stitches. Work Rib Pattern as for back, increase 1 stitch on last (WS) row—54 (58, 62) stitches. Change to larger needles. Work Chart Pattern, beginning and ending as indicated for sleeve, AT SAME TIME, increase 1 stitch each side (working increases into pattern) on 5th row, then every 6th (4th, 4th) row 18 (19, 17) times, then every 8th (6th, 6th) row 2 (7, 7) times—96 (112, 112) stitches. Piece measures approximately 20½ (19½, 19)" from beginning. Work 1¼ (1½, 2¼)" even. Bind off.

Finishing

Block pieces. Sew shoulders.

Collar

With RS facing, smaller circular needle and MC, begin at center front and pick up and knit 55 (55, 57) stitches evenly along right front neck, 41 (41, 47) stitches along back neck, and 55 (55, 57) stitches along left front neck—151 (151, 161) stitches. Turn work. *Begin Rib Pattern: Row 1* (WS) * P1, k1; repeat from *, end p1. Continue in rib pattern as established until collar measures 2", end with a WS row. Change to larger circular needle.

Shape collar

Begin short-row shaping: Row 1 (RS) Work 107 (107, 113) stitches, wrap next stitch as for a purl stitch and turn (W&T). *Row 2* Work 62 (62, 64) stitches, W&T. *Row 3* Work 58 (58, 60) stitches, W&T. *Row 4* Work 54 (54, 56) stitches, W&T. *Row 5* Work 50 (50, 52) stitches, W&T. *Row 6* Work 46 (46, 48) stitches, W&T. *Row 7* Work 42 (42, 44) stitches, W&T. *Row 8* Work 38 (38, 40) stitches, W&T. *Row 9* Work 34 (34, 36) stitches, W&T. *Row 10* Work 30 (30, 32) stitches, W&T. *Rows 11 and 12* Work to end of row, hiding purl wraps as you come to them. Work even in rib pattern until collar at center back measures 4¾ (5, 5¼)". Change to CC and work 2 more rows. Bind off in rib. Lay left collar over right collar at center front and sew edges in place.

Set in sleeves. Sew side and sleeve seams.

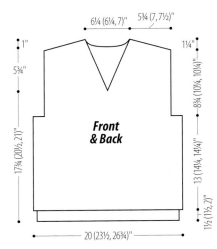

Chart Pattern

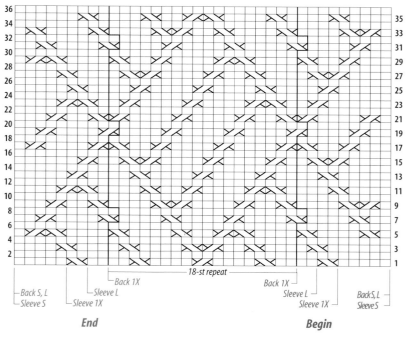

18-st repeat

Back S, L
Sleeve S

Sleeve 1X

Sleeve L

Back 1X

Back 1X

Sleeve L

Sleeve 1X

Back S, L
Sleeve S

End

Begin

Stitch key

☐ Knit on RS, purl on WS

☒ **1/1 RT** Sl 1 to cn, hold to back, sl next stitch purlwise with yarn in back (wyib); k 1 from cn.

☒ **1/1 LT** Sl 1 to cn, hold to front, k1; sl stitch from cn purlwise wyib.

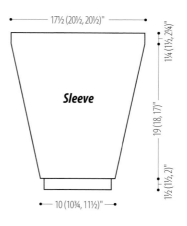

17½ (20½, 20½)"

1¼ (1½, 2¾)"

Sleeve

19 (18, 17)"

1½ (1½, 2)"

10 (10¾, 11½)"

Off to the pub with the guys, to the game with the kids, or to the movies with you: this is one sweater he'll be proud to wear, anywhere. The easiest of guernsey patterning is simple, clean, and modern. The sleeves reverse the knits and purls of the body pattern for additional interest.

Norah Gaughan

Mandalay Turtle

EASY

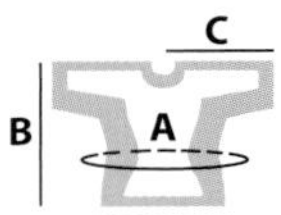

LOOSE FIT

Shown in Extra Large
Sizes S (M, L, 1X, 2X)
A 41 (45, 49, 53½, 57½)"
B 24 (25, 25, 25, 27)"
C 31 (32, 33, 34, 35)"

10cm/4"

28

19

• over Body Pattern, using larger needles

1 2 3 **4** 5 6

• **Medium weight**
• 1425 (1575, 1700, 1800, 2025) yds

• 3.5mm/US 4 and 4mm/US 6,
or size to obtain gauge

• 3.5mm/US 4, 40cm/16" long

&

• stitch holders
• stitch markers

original yarn

REYNOLDS Mandalay (silk; 50g; 95yds) Earth

Note
See *School*, page 82, for 3-needle bind-off.

Rib Pattern
MULTIPLE OF 5 STITCHES, PLUS 2
Row 1 (RS) * K2, p3; repeat from *, end k2. *Row 2* * P2, k3; repeat from *, end p2. Repeat Rows 1 and 2 for Rib Pattern.

Body Pattern
MULTIPLE OF 5 STITCHES, PLUS 2
Row 1 (RS) Knit. *Row 2* * K2, p3; repeat from *, end k2. Repeat Rows 1 and 2 for Body Pattern.

Sleeve Pattern
MULTIPLE OF 5 STITCHES, PLUS 2
Row 1 (RS) * K2, p3; repeat from *, end k2. *Row 2* Knit. Repeat Rows 1 and 2 for Sleeve Pattern.

Back
* With smaller needles, cast on 97 (107, 117, 127, 137) stitches. Work in Rib Pattern for 4 rows. Change to larger needles. Work in Body Pattern until piece measures 15 (15½, 15, 14½, 16)" from beginning, end with a WS row. Place a marker at each end of row to mark armholes. Work even until armhole measures 6¼ (6¾, 7¼, 7¾, 8¼)" above markers, end with a RS row, decreasing 4 (6, 6, 6, 8) stitches evenly across last row—93 (101, 111, 121, 129) stitches. * Knit every row for 24 rows more. Armhole measures approximately 9 (9½, 10, 10½, 11)". Place stitches on hold.

Front
Work from * to * as for back. Continue as for back, AT SAME TIME, shape neck as follows:
Shape neck
Next row (WS) K41 (44, 48, 52, 56) stitches, join 2nd ball of yarn and bind off center 11 (13, 15, 17, 17) stitches, knit to end. Working both sides at same time, bind off from each neck edge 4 stitches once, 3 stitches once, 2 stitches once, 1 stitch once—31 (34, 38, 42, 46) stitches each side. Work even until armhole measures same length as back. Place stitches on hold.

Sleeves
With smaller needles, cast on 47 (47, 52, 52, 52) stitches. Work in Rib Pattern for 1½", end with a WS row. Change to larger needles. Work in Sleeve Pattern, AT SAME TIME, increase 1 stitch each side (working increases into pattern) on 5th row, then every 6th (4th, 6th, 4th, 4th) row 10 (1, 18, 7, 13) times, every 8th (6th, 8th, 6th, 6th) row 8 (20, 2, 16, 12) times—85 (91, 94, 100, 104) stitches. Knit every row for 6 rows. Piece measures approximately 20¾" from beginning. Bind off purlwise.

Finishing
Block pieces. Join shoulders, using 3-needle bind-off, as follows: Join 31 (34, 38, 42, 46) stitches of first shoulder, bind off back neck stitches until 31 (34, 38, 42, 46) stitches remain, then join stitches of 2nd shoulder.
Neckband
With RS facing and circular needle, begin at left shoulder and pick up and knit 49 (51, 53, 55, 55) stitches evenly along front neck and 31 (33, 35, 37, 37) stitches along back neck—80 (84, 88, 92, 92) stitches. Place marker, join and work in rounds of k2, p2 rib for 6". Bind off in rib.
Sew top of sleeves between armhole markers. Sew side and sleeve seams.

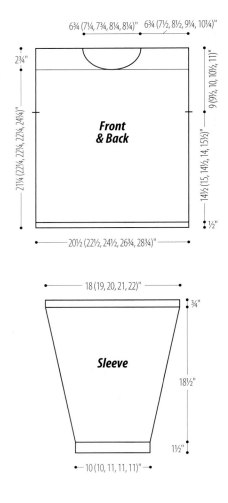

6¾ (7¼, 7¾, 8¼, 8¼)" 6¾ (7½, 8½, 9¼, 10¼)"

2¾"

9 (9½, 10, 10½, 11)"

21¼ (22¼, 22¾, 22¼, 24¼)"

Front & Back

14½ (15, 14½, 14, 15½)"

½"

20½ (22½, 24½, 26¾, 28¾)"

18 (19, 20, 21, 22)"

¾"

Sleeve

18½"

1½"

10 (10, 11, 11, 11)"

The classic pullover gets some new details: seed stitch borders and garter pinstripes give this favorite relaxed silhouette a crisp touch. Add a distinctive band of duplicate stitching across the chest in your favorite contrasting color.

Georgina Estefania

Cypress Needle Crew

INTERMEDIATE

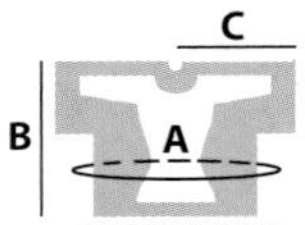

OVERSIZED FIT

Shown in Large
L (1X, 2X, 3X)
A 47½ (52, 58½, 63)"
B 26 (26½, 27, 27½)"
C 32½ (33, 34, 34½)"

10cm/4"

30
21

• over stockinette stitch (knit on RS, purl on WS), using larger needles

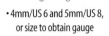
1 2 3 **4** 5 6

• **Medium weight**
MC • 1850 (2050, 2225, 2425) yds
CC • 150 yds

• 4mm/US 6 and 5mm/US 8, or size to obtain gauge

• 4 mm/US 6, 40cm/16" long

&

• stitch markers
• yarn needle

original yarn

BARUFFA Maratona (wool; 50g; 121 yds)
Brown (MC) and Gray (CC)

Notes

1 See *School*, page 82, for duplicate stitch. **2** Work front with MC only, then work duplicate stitch with CC over 15 rows of stockinette stitch after piece is complete.

Seed stitch

ODD NUMBER OF STITCHES

Row 1 P1, * k1, p1; repeat from *. *Row 2* Knit the purl stitches and purl the knit stitches. Repeat Row 2 for Seed stitch.

Back

With smaller needles and MC, cast on 125 (137, 153, 165) stitches. Work in Seed stitch for 2", end with a RS row. Change to larger needles. *Begin Stitch Pattern: Row 1* (WS) Purl. *Row 2* K6 (12, 4, 10), [p1, k15] 7 (7, 9, 9) times, p1, k6 (12, 4, 10). Repeat Rows 1 and 2 until piece measures 26 (26½, 27, 27½)" from beginning. Bind off.

Front

Work as for back until piece measures 18½ (18¾, 19, 19¼)" from beginning, end with a RS row. [Purl 1 row, knit 1 row] 7 times, purl 1 row. (Work duplicate stitch, following chart, over these 15 rows of stockinette stitch when piece is complete.) Beginning with row 2, continue in Stitch Pattern until piece measures 22¾ (23¼, 23¾, 24¼)" from beginning, end with a WS row.

Shape neck

Next row (RS) Work 54 (59, 66, 71) stitches, join 2nd ball of yarn and bind off center 17 (19, 21, 23) stitches, work to end. Working both sides at same time, bind off from each neck edge 4 stitches once, 3 stitches once, 2 stitches 1 (2, 2, 2) times, 1 stitch 2 (1, 1, 1) times—43 (47, 54, 59) stitches each side. Work even until piece measures same length as back to shoulder. Bind off.

Sleeves

With smaller needles and MC, cast on 49 (53, 57, 61) stitches. Work in Seed stitch for 2", end with a RS row. Change to larger needles. *Begin Stitch Pattern: Row 1* (WS) Purl. *Row 2* K0 (2, 4, 6), [p1, k15] 3 times, p1, k0 (2, 4, 6). Continue

in pattern as established, AT SAME TIME, increase 1 stitch each side (working increases into pattern) every 4th row 18 (23, 25, 30) times, every 6th row 10 (6, 4, 0) times—105 (111, 115, 121) stitches. Work even until piece measures 20½ (20, 19½, 19)" from beginning. Bind off.

Finishing

Block pieces.
Work duplicate stitch
With CC, work duplicate stitch over 15 rows of stockinette stitch of front, following chart for placement. Sew shoulders.
Neckband
With RS facing, circular needle and MC, begin at shoulder seam and pick up and knit 113 (121, 127, 133) stitches evenly around neck edge. Place marker, join, and work Seed stitch in rounds for 1¼". Bind off loosely purlwise.
Place markers 10 (10½, 11, 11½)" down from shoulders on front and back for armholes. Sew top of sleeves between markers. Sew side and sleeve seams.

Color key
▨ MC
▨ Duplicate stitch with CC

Stitch key
▤ Vertical columns of garter stitch in stitch pattern

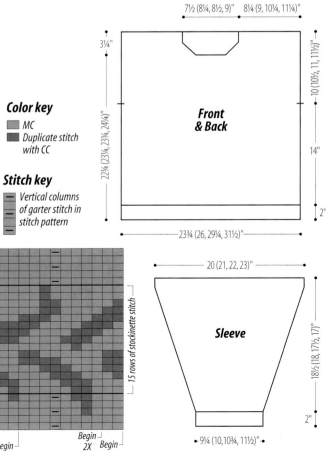

7½ (8¼, 8½, 9)"   8¼ (9, 10¼, 11¼)"

3¼"

10 (10½, 11, 11½)"

22¾ (23¼, 23¾, 24¼)"

Front & Back

14"

2"

23¾ (26, 29¼, 31½)"

20 (21, 22, 23)"

Sleeve

18½ (18, 17½, 17)"

2"

9¼ (10, 10¾, 11½)"

Duplicate stitch chart *(showing placement of duplicate stitch motifs in 15 stockinette stitch rows of front)*

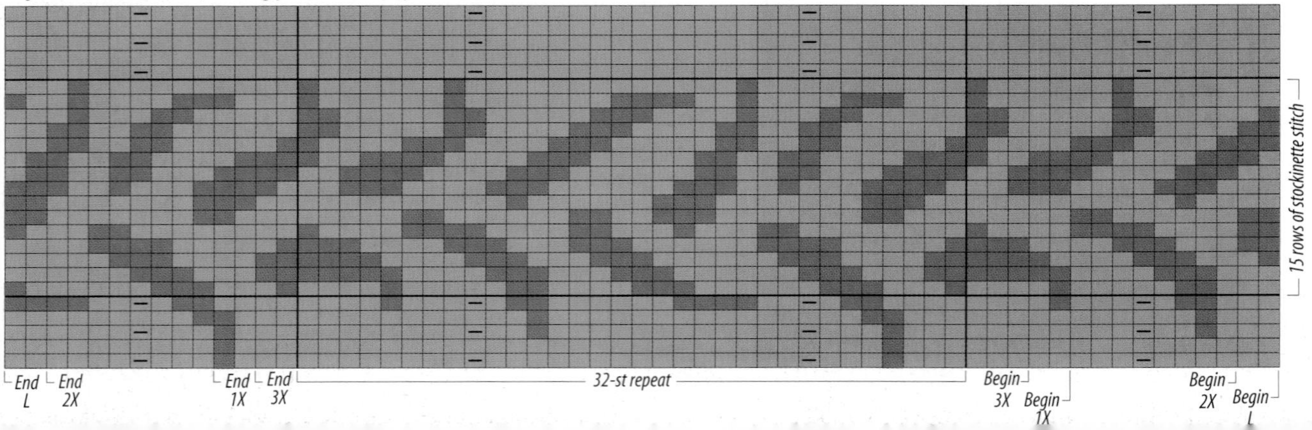

15 rows of stockinette stitch

End L   End 2X   End 1X   End 3X   32-st repeat   Begin 3X   Begin 1X   Begin 2X   Begin L

Earthy brown and tan glow in this gent's sweater that features a marquetry-inspired center panel. The silk tweed yarn adds polish to a casual style.

Barbara Venishnick

Bayou Gold

INTERMEDIATE

C

B — A

OVERSIZED FIT

Shown in Large
M (L, 1X, 2X)

A 47½ (52½, 55, 58½)"
B 26 (26½, 27, 27½)"
C 31½ (32½, 33, 34)"

17cm/6 ¾"

33
• over center panel chart

10cm/4"

26

17
• over stockinette stitch
(knit on RS, purl on WS)

1 2 3 **4** 5 6

• Medium weight
MC • 1100 (1200, 1300, 1450) yds
CC • 500 (500, 600, 600) yds

• 4mm/US 6, or size to obtain gauge,
40cm/16" and 74cm/29" long

3.75mm/F

&

• stitch marker
• stitch holders

original yarn

ROWAN YARNS Summer Tweed (silk, cotton;
50g; 118 yds) in Rafia (MC) and Reed (CC)

Notes

1 See *School*, page 82 for SSK and crochet chain stitch. **2** Center panels for front and back are worked from the bottom up to shoulder; garter strips are picked up, joining front and back panels, and worked outward; sides of body front and back are continued out to side seam, and sleeves are worked to cuff.

Center Back Panel

With MC, cast on 33 stitches. Work 20 rows of Center Panel Chart 10 (10, 10, 11) times, then work rows 1–8 (1–12, 1–16, 0) once more. Piece measures approximately 24½ (25, 25½, 26)" from beginning. Place stitches on hold.

Center Front Panel

Work as for back panel until 20 rows of chart have been worked 9 times, then work first 2 (6, 2, 6) rows once more. Piece measures approximately 21½ (22, 21½, 22)" from beginning.

Shape neck

Next row (RS) Work 6 stitches, place center 21 stitches on hold, join 2nd ball of yarn and work last 6 stitches. Working both sides at same time, decrease 1 stitch at each neck edge every other row 5 times. Place remaining stitch each side on crochet hook and chain 7 (7, 11, 11) stitches. Fasten off.

Right Side Garter Strip

With RS facing, longer needle and CC, pick up and knit 104 (106, 108, 110) stitches evenly along right edge of center back panel, place marker for top of shoulder, then with RS of center front panel facing, pick up 1 stitch in each of the 7 (7, 11, 11) chains of right front neck (joining front and back panels), then pick up and knit 97 (99, 97, 99) stitches along remainder of front panel—208 (212, 216, 220) stitches. Knit 15 rows. Cut CC. Change to MC and stockinette stitch.

Right Side and Sleeve

Shape shoulder

Next row (RS) Knit to 3 stitches before shoulder marker, k2tog, k1, slip marker, k1, SSK, knit to end. Repeat decrease row every 8th row 5 (6, 6, 7) times more—196 (198, 202, 204) stitches. Work 3 (3, 7, 5) rows even, removing shoulder marker.

Shape sleeve

Bind off 50 (51, 52, 53) stitches at beginning of next 2 rows—96 (96, 98, 98) stitches. Work 4 rows even. *Next (decrease) row* (RS) K1, SSK, knit to last 3 stitches, k2tog, k1. Repeat decrease row every 6th row 18 times more—58 (58, 60, 60) stitches. Work 1 row even. Sleeve measures approximately 18" from beginning. Cut MC. Change to CC.

Cuff

Next row (RS) Knit, decreasing 14 stitches evenly across—44 (44, 46, 46) stitches. Knit 13 rows more. Bind off.

Left Side and Sleeve

Work as for right side, picking up 97 (99, 97, 99) stitches for garter strip along center front panel, then 1 stitch in each of the 7 (7, 11, 11) chains of left front neck, then 104 (106, 108, 110) stitches along left side of center back panel—208 (212, 216, 220) stitches.

Finishing

Block piece. Sew right side and sleeve seam.

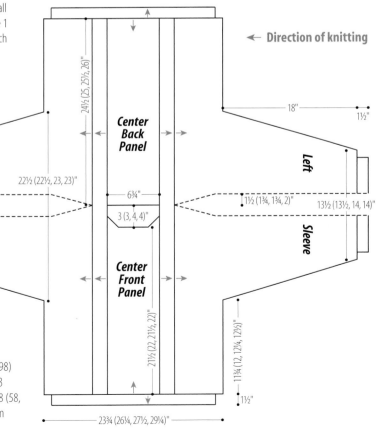

← **Direction of knitting**

Center Back Panel

Center Front Panel

Sleeve

Right

Sleeve

Left

24½ (25, 25½, 26)"

22½ (22½, 23, 23)"

6¾"

3 (3, 4, 4)"

21½ (22, 21½, 22)"

18"

1½"

1½ (1¾, 1¾, 2)"

13½ (13½, 14, 14)"

11¾ (12, 12¼, 12½)"

1½"

23¾ (26¼, 27½, 29¼)"

Lower edge band

With RS facing, longer needle and CC, begin at left side seam and pick up and knit 76 (89, 94, 104) stitches evenly along lower edge of back, then 76 (89, 94, 104) stitches along front—152 (178, 188, 208) stitches. Knit 13 rows. Bind off. Sew left side and sleeve seam.

Neckband

With RS facing, shorter needle and CC, knit 33 stitches from back neck holder, then pick up and knit 1 stitch in each of 7 (7, 11, 11) chain stitches at left front neck, 6 stitches along side neck decreases, knit 21 stitches from front neck holder, pick up and knit 6 stitches along side neck decreases at right front neck, then 1 stitch in each of 7 (7, 11, 11) chain stitches—80 (80, 88, 88) stitches. Place marker, join, and [purl 1 round, knit 1 round] 5 times. Then knit every round for 1". Bind off loosely. Fold stockinette stitch portion of band to inside and sew in place.

Center Panel Chart

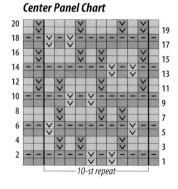

10-st repeat

Stitch key

☐ K on RS, p on WS
– K on WS
∨ Sl 1 purlwise with yarn at WS of work

Color key

▢ MC
▢ CC

Linda Cyr

If you're having trouble deciding on a sweater to knit, take a good look at this one. It can't be beat for comfortable wearing and easy, traditional patterns. The patterns are easy to memorize, and the knitting goes fairly quickly. Design details such as the pocket, the cables in the ribbing, and the diamonds running up the saddle shoulders hallmark this as a handknit.

Kangaroo Pockets

INTERMEDIATE +

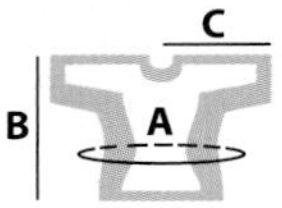

LOOSE FIT

Shown in Large
Sizes S (M, L, 1X, 2X/3X)
A 42½ (46½, 51, 55½, 60)"
B 27¼"
C 32 (33, 34, 35, 36)"

10cm/4"
28
22
• over Moss stitch

1 2 3 **4** 5 6
• Medium weight
• 1850 (2000, 2150, 2400, 2500) yds

• 4.5mm/US 7, or size to obtain gauge

&
• stitch holders
• stitch markers
• cable needle (cn)

original yarn

CLASSIC ELITE Waterspun
(wool; 50g; 137yds) Camel

Note
See *School*, page 82, for Make 1 (M1) and knit in row below.

Moss stitch *ANY NUMBER OF STITCHES*
Row 1 (RS) * K1, p1; repeat from *. *Rows 2 and 4* Knit the knit stitches and purl the purl stitches. *Row 3* * P1, k1; repeat from *. Repeat Rows 1–4 for Moss stitch.

Back
Cast on 126 (138, 150, 162, 174) stitches. *Begin Rib pattern and Charts A and B: Row 1* (RS) P2 (0, 2, 0, 2), [k2, p2] 4 (6, 7, 9, 10) times, work 4 stitches Chart A, [p2, k2] 5 times, p2, [4 stitches Chart A, p2, k2, p2] twice, k2, p2, [4 stitches Chart B, p2, k2, p2] twice, [k2, p2] 4 times, 4 stitches Chart B, [p2, k2] 4 (6, 7, 9, 10) times, p2 (0, 2, 0, 2). *Row 2* K2 (0, 2, 0, 2), [p2, k2] 4 (6, 7, 9, 10) times, work 4 stitches Chart B, [k2, p2] 5 times, k2, [4 stitches Chart B, k2, p2, k2] twice, p2, k2, [4 stitches Chart A, k2, p2, k2] twice, [p2, k2] 4 times, 4 stitches Chart A, [k2, p2] 4 (6, 7, 9, 10) times, k2 (0, 2, 0, 2). Continue in patterns as established for 13 rows more. *Next row* (WS) Work 58 (64, 70, 76, 82) stitches in pattern, k2tog, p2, k2, p2, k2tog, work in pattern to end—124 (136, 148, 160, 172) stitches. *Begin Moss stitch and Charts C and D: Row 1* (RS) Work in Moss stitch over 17 (23, 29, 35, 41) stitches, p1, work 4 stitches Chart A, p1, work Chart C over 20 stitches, p1, 4 stitches Chart A, 28 stitches Chart D, 4 stitches Chart B, p1, Chart C over 20 stitches, p1, 4 stitches Chart B, p1, work Moss stitch over 17 (23, 29, 35, 41) stitches. *Row 2* Work 17 (23, 29, 35, 41) stitches in Moss stitch, k1, 4 stitches Chart B, k1, 20 stitches Chart C, k1, 4 stitches Chart B, 28 stitches Chart D, 4 stitches Chart A, k1, 20 stitches Chart C, k1, 4 stitches Chart A, k1, work 17 (23, 29, 35, 41) stitches in Moss stitch. Continue in patterns as established until piece measures approximately 17¾ (17¾, 17¼, 16¾, 16¾)" from beginning, end with row 52 (52, 48, 44, 44) of Chart D.
Shape armholes
Bind off 6 (6, 6, 7, 8) stitches at beginning of next 2 rows. Decrease 1 stitch each side every row 5 times, then every other row 2 (2, 2, 3, 4) times, every 4th row twice, every 6th row twice—90 (102, 114, 122, 130) stitches. Work even until armhole measures approximately 7½ (7½, 8, 8½, 8½)", end with row 48 of Chart D.
Shape shoulders and neck
Bind off 26 (32, 38, 42, 46) stitches at beginning of next 2 rows—38 stitches. Work 6 rows even. Bind off.

Pocket lining
Cast on 83 stitches. Beginning with Row 3, work in Moss stitch for 15 rows, ending with Row 1. Place stitches on hold.

Front
Work as for back until there are 14 rows above ribbing.
Divide for pocket flap
Next row (RS) Work 17 (23, 29, 35, 41) stitches in pattern and place these stitches on hold, work next 90 stitches, then place remaining 17 (23, 29, 35, 41) stitches on hold. Continue working center 90 stitches until pocket flap measures 6", end with a WS row. Place stitches on hold.

Join pocket lining
With RS facing, join yarn to stitches on holder after pocket flap and work 17 (23, 29, 35, 41) stitches of right front as follows: Work 1 row even. *Next row* (WS) Work 17 (23, 29, 35, 41) stitches, then continue Moss stitch over 83 pocket lining stitches, then over 17 (23, 29, 35, 41) left front stitches on holder—117 (129, 141, 153, 165) stitches. Continue in Moss stitch until pocket lining is even with pocket flap, end with a WS row.

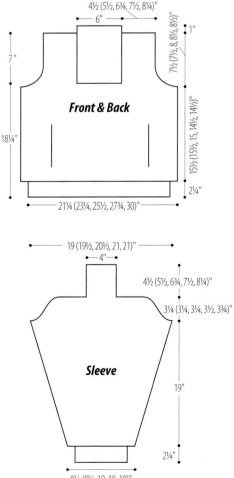

4½ (5½, 6¾, 7½, 8¼)"

6"

7½ (7½, 8, 8½, 8½)"

1"

7"

Front & Back

18¼"

15½ (15½, 15, 14½, 14½)"

2¼"

21¼ (23¼, 25½, 27¾, 30)"

19 (19½, 20½, 21, 21)"

4"

4½ (5½, 6¾, 7½, 8¼)"

3¼ (3¼, 3¼, 3½, 3¾)"

Sleeve

19"

2¼"

8½ (8½, 10, 10, 10)"

Join pocket flap and lining

Next row (RS) Work 17 (23, 29, 35, 41) stitches in pattern, then work center 90 stitches as follows: work 83 stitches of pocket lining together with 83 stitches of pocket flap (working the extra 7 pocket flap stitches alone at evenly spaced intervals across), work to end—124 (136, 148, 160, 172) stitches. Continue in patterns until piece measures same length as back to underarm. Shape armholes as for back, AT SAME TIME, after 4 (4, 8, 12, 12) rows of armhole shaping have been worked and armhole measures ½ (½, 1, 1½, 1½)", work as follows: mark center 36 stitches.

Shape neck

Next row (RS) Work to center marked stitches, join 2nd ball of yarn and bind off 36 stitches, work to end. Working both sides at same time, continue to shape armholes at each side as for back—27 (33, 39, 43, 47) stitches each side (1 stitch more than back shoulders). Work even until armhole measures same length as back to shoulder.

Shape shoulders

Bind off 27 (33, 39, 43, 47) stitches at beginning of next 2 rows.

Right Sleeve

Cast on 44 (44, 52, 52, 52) stitches. *Begin Rib pattern and Charts A and B: Row 1* (RS) [P2, k2] 2 (2, 3, 3, 3) times, p2, work 4 stitches Chart A, p2, k2, p2, [4 stitches Chart B, p2, k2, p2] twice, [k2, p2] 1 (1, 2, 2, 2) times. Continue in patterns as established for 14 rows more. *Increase row* (WS) * [K1, M1, k1, p2] 2 (2, 3, 3, 3) times, k1, M1, k1 *, work in pattern across next 24 stitches, work from * to * once—50 (50, 60, 60, 60) stitches. *Begin Moss stitch and Chart E: Row 1* (RS) Work 12 (12, 17, 17, 17) stitches in Moss stitch, p1, 4 stitches Chart A, 16 stitches Chart E, 4 stitches Chart B, p1, 12 (12, 17, 17, 17) stitches in Moss stitch. Continue in patterns as established, AT SAME TIME, increase 1 stitch each side (working increases into Moss stitch) every 4th row 24 (30, 21, 27, 27) times, every 6th row 5 (1, 7, 3, 3) times—108 (112, 116, 120, 120) stitches. Work even until piece measures 21¼" from beginning, end with a WS row.

Shape cap and sleeve saddle

Bind off 6 (6, 6, 7, 8) stitches at beginning of next 2 rows. Decrease 1 stitch each side every row 5 (5, 5, 3, 3) times, then every other row 5 (5, 5, 7, 10) times, then every row 5 (5, 5, 5, 1) times. Bind off 20 (22, 24, 25, 25) stitches at beginning of next 2 rows—26 stitches. Work even until saddle measures 4½ (5½, 6¾, 7½, 8¼)". Bind off.

Left Sleeve

Cast on 44 (44, 52, 52, 52) stitches. *Begin Rib pattern and Charts A and B: Row 1* (RS) [P2, k2] 2 (2, 3, 3, 3) times, p2, [work 4 stitches Chart A, p2, k2, p2] twice, 4 stitches Chart B, [p2, k2] 2 (2, 3, 3, 3) times, p2. Complete to correspond to right sleeve, except work Chart F in place of Chart E.

Finishing

Block pieces.

Collar

Cast on 34 stitches. Knit 1 row. *Begin Rib pattern: Row 1* K2, * k1, k1 in row below next stitch on left needle; repeat from *, end k2. Repeat Row 1 until collar measures 26". Bind off.

Sew sleeve saddles to front and back shoulders (see Assembly Diagram). Sew sides of 1" back neck extension along 1" at top of saddle. Set in sleeves. Sew side and sleeve seams. Using photo as guide, sew collar around neck edge, overlapping left over right at center front.

Chart A
4 sts

Chart B
4 sts

Chart C
4-st repeat

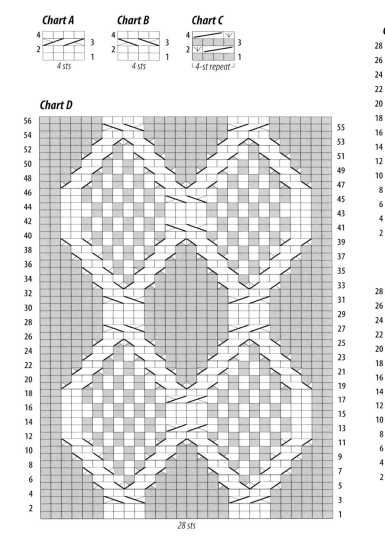

28 sts

Chart E

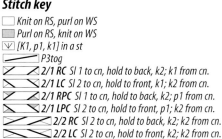

16 sts

Chart F

16 sts

Assembly Diagram

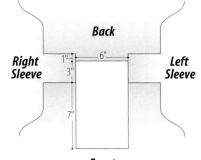

Back

Right Sleeve

Left Sleeve

Front

6"

1"

3"

7"

Stitch key

☐ Knit on RS, purl on WS
▨ Purl on RS, knit on WS
▽ [K1, p1, k1] in a st
P3tog
2/1 RC Sl 1 to cn, hold to back, k2; k1 from cn.
2/1 LC Sl 2 to cn, hold to front, k1; k2 from cn.
2/1 RPC Sl 1 to cn, hold to back, k2; p1 from cn.
2/1 LPC Sl 2 to cn, hold to front, p1; k2 from cn.
2/2 RC Sl 2 to cn, hold to back, k2; k2 from cn.
2/2 LC Sl 2 to cn, hold to front, k2; k2 from cn.

Sleeve Patterns

12 (12, 17, 17, 17) sts Moss st	1 st Rev St st	4 sts Chart B	16 sts Chart E or F	4 sts Chart A	1 st Rev St st	12 (12, 17, 17, 17) sts Moss st
			^Center			

Body Patterns

17 (23, 29, 35, 41) sts Moss st	1 st Rev St st	4 sts Chart B	1 st Rev St st	20 sts Chart C	1 st Rev St st	4 sts Chart B	28 sts Chart D	4 sts Chart A	1 st Rev St st	20 sts Chart C	1 st Rev St st	4 sts Chart A	1 st Rev St st	17 (23, 29, 35, 41) sts Moss st
							^Center							

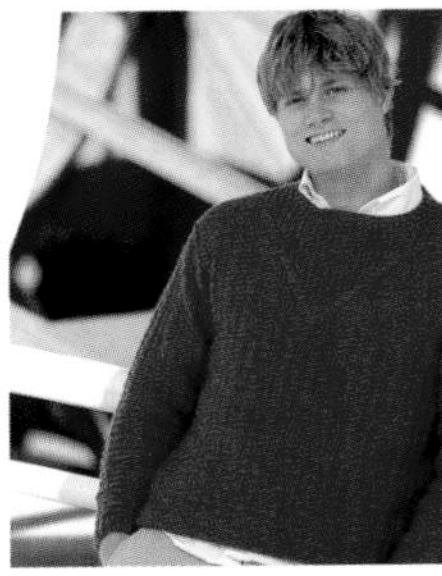

Any guy will welcome this cashmere blend sweater. The ribbed texture and V-yoke cable are handsome details.

Kathy Zimmerman

Colorado River

INTERMEDIATE +

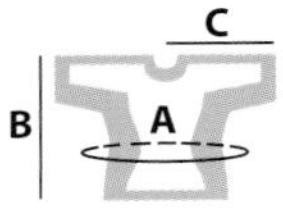
C
B
A
LOOSE FIT

Shown in Medium
S (M, L, 1X, 2X)
A 40½ (44½, 48½, 52½, 56½)"
B 22¾ (24, 25, 25¾, 26¾)"
C 32 (33, 34, 35, 36)"

10cm/4"
40
24
• ***over Chart A, using larger needles***

1 2 **3** 4 5 6

• ***Light weight***
• 1725 (1925, 2150, 2300, 2500) yds

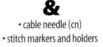

• 3.75mm/US 5 and 4mm/US 6, or size to obtain gauge

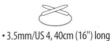

• 3.5mm/US 4, 40cm (16") long

&

• cable needle (cn)
• stitch markers and holders

original yarn

SR KERTZER COLLECTION Truffles (wool, cashmere; 25g; 81 yds) Red

Note

See *School*, page 82, for SSP, Make 1 Knit (M1K) and Purl (M1P), and 3-needle bind-off.

Back

With smaller needles, cast on 121 (133, 145, 157, 169) stitches. ***Begin Rib Pattern***: ***Row 1*** (WS) K0 (0, 2, 2, 0), [p1, k3] 1 (0, 1, 0, 2) times, [p3, k3, p1, k3] 11 (13, 13, 15, 16) times, p3 (3, 3, 3, 1), [k3, p1] 1 (0, 1, 0, 0) time, k0 (0, 2, 2, 0). Continue in rib pattern as established until ribbing measures 1¼", end with a WS row. Change to larger needles. Beginning and ending as indicated for back, work Chart A until piece measures approximately 14¾ (15½, 16, 16¾, 17¼)" from beginning, end with chart row 4.

Shape armholes

Continue Chart A pattern as established, bind off 10 (12, 15, 17, 19) stitches at beginning of next 2 rows—101 (109, 115, 123, 131) stitches. ***Begin Yoke Pattern: Next row*** (RS) Work 47 (51, 54, 58, 62) stitches, p1, M1K, k1, M1K, k3, M1K, k1, M1K, p1, work to end—105 (113, 119, 127, 135) stitches. ***Next row*** Work 47 (51, 54, 58, 62) stitches, k1, place marker (pm), [M1P, p1] twice, M1P, p5, [M1P, p1] twice, M1P, pm, k1, work to end—111 (119, 125, 133, 141) stitches. ***Begin Charts B and C, and K1, P2 Rib Pattern: Row 1*** (RS) Work to 1 stitch before marker, p1, slip marker (sm), work 6 stitches Chart B, p1, k1, p1, work 6 stitches Chart C, sm, p1, work to end. ***Row 2*** Work to 1 stitch before marker, k1, sm, work 6 stitches Chart C, k1, p1, k1, 6 stitches Chart B, sm, k1, work to end. ***Row 3*** Work to 2 stitches before marker, SSP, sm, work 6 stitches Chart B, M1P, p1, k1, p1, M1P, 6 stitches Chart C, sm, p2tog, work to end. ***Row 4*** Work to 1 stitch before marker, k1, sm, 6 stitches Chart C, k2, p1, k2, 6 stitches Chart B, sm, k1, work to end. ***Row 5*** Work to 2 stitches before marker, SSP, sm, 6 stitches Chart B, M1P, p2, k1, p2, M1P, 6 stitches Chart C, sm, p2tog, work to end. ***Row 6*** Work to 1 stitch before marker, k1, sm, 6 stitches Chart C, k3, p1, k3, 6 stitches Chart B, sm, k1, work to end. ***Row 7*** Work to 2 stitches before marker, SSP, sm, 6 stitches Chart B, M1P, [k1, p2] twice, k1, M1P, 6 stitches Chart C, sm, p2tog, work to end. ***Row 8*** Work to 1 stitch before marker, k1, sm, 6 stitches Chart C, k1, [p1, k2] twice, p1, k1, 6 stitches Chart B, sm, k1, work to end. ***Row 9*** Work to 2 stitches before marker, SSP, sm, 6 stitches Chart B, M1P, p1, [k1, p2] twice, k1, p1, M1P, 6 stitches Chart C, sm, p2tog, work to end. ***Row 10*** Work to 1 stitch before marker, k1, sm, 6 stitches Chart C, k2, [p1, k2] 3 times, 6 stitches Chart B, sm, k1, work to end. ***Row 11*** Work to 2 stitches before marker, SSP, sm, 6 stitches Chart B, M1P, p2, [k1, p2] 3 times, M1P, 6 stitches Chart C, sm, p2tog, work to end. ***Row 12*** Work to 1 stitch before marker, k1, sm, 6 stitches Chart C, k3, [p1, k2] 3 times, k1, 6 stitches Chart B, sm, k1, work to end. Continue in patterns as established, working yoke increase stitches into rib pattern, until armhole measures 8 (8½, 9, 9, 9½)", end with a WS row. Place stitches on hold.

Front

Work as for back until armhole measures 5¼ (5¾, 6¼, 6¼, 6¾)", end with a WS row.

Shape neck

Next row (RS) Work 43 (47, 50, 54, 58) stitches in pattern as established, join 2nd ball of yarn and bind off center 25 stitches, work to end. Working both sides at same time, bind off from each neck edge 3 stitches 1 (1, 1, 1, 2) times, 2 stitches 1 (2, 2, 3, 2) times, 1 stitch 4 (3, 3, 2, 2) times—34 (37, 40, 43, 46) stitches each side. Work even until armhole measures same length as back to shoulder. Place stitches on hold.

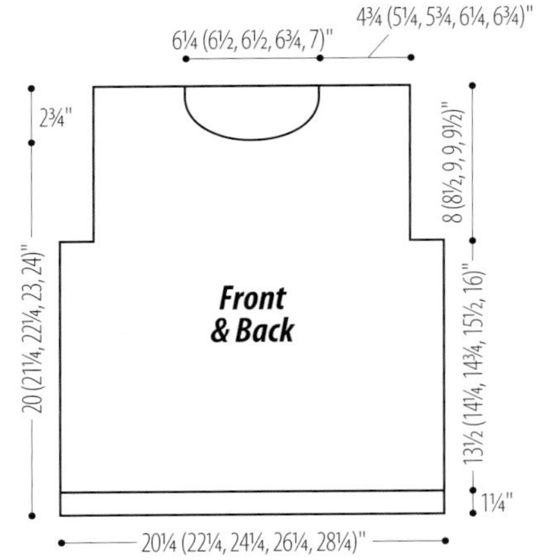
4¾ (5¼, 5¾, 6¼, 6¾)"
6¼ (6½, 6½, 6¾, 7)"
2¾"
8 (8½, 9, 9, 9½)"
20 (21¼, 22¼, 23, 24)"
Front & Back
13½ (14¼, 14¾, 15½, 16)"
1¼"
20¼ (22¼, 24¼, 26¼, 28¼)"

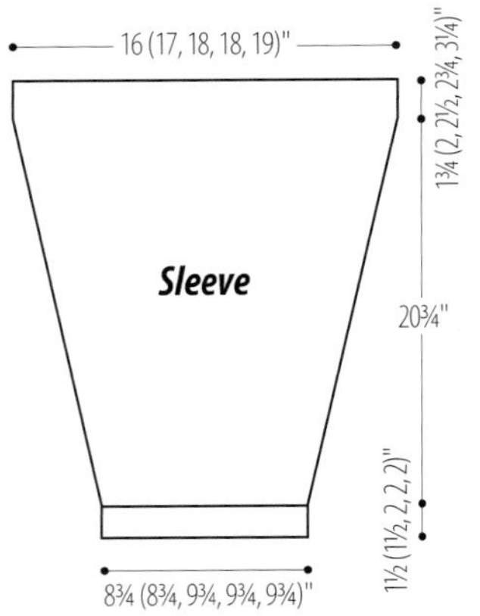
16 (17, 18, 18, 19)"
1¾ (2, 2½, 2¾, 3¼)"
Sleeve
20¾"
1½ (1½, 2, 2, 2)"
8¾ (8¾, 9¾, 9¾, 9¾)"

Sleeves

With smaller needles, cast on 53 (53, 59, 59, 59) stitches. *Begin Rib Pattern: Row 1* (WS) K0 (0, 3, 3, 3), [p3, k3, p1, k3] 5 times, p3, k0 (0, 3, 3, 3). Continue in rib pattern as established until ribbing measures 1½ (1½, 2, 2, 2)", end with a WS row. Change to larger needles. Beginning and ending as indicated for sleeve, work Chart A, AT SAME TIME, increase 1 stitch each side (working increases into pattern), on 7th row, then every 8th (8th, 8th, 8th, 6th) row 5 (20, 20, 20, 8) times, every 10th (10th, 10th, 10th, 8th) row 16 (4, 4, 4, 19) times—97 (103, 109, 109, 115) stitches. Piece measures approximately 22¼ (22¼, 22¾, 22¾, 22¾)" from beginning. Work even for 1¾ (2, 2½, 2¾, 3¼)". Bind off.

Finishing

Block pieces. Join shoulders, using 3-needle bind-off, as follows: join 34 (37, 40, 43, 46) stitches of first shoulder, bind off stitches for back neck until 34 (37, 40, 43, 46) stitches remain, join 2nd shoulder.

Neckband

With RS facing and circular needle, begin at left shoulder and pick up and knit 23 (25, 25, 27, 29) stitches evenly along left front neck, 25 stitches along center front neck, 23 (25, 25, 27, 29) stitches along right front neck, and 43 (45, 45, 47, 49) stitches along back neck—114 (120, 120, 126, 132) stitches. Pm, join, and work in rib pattern as follows: *Round 1* P2 (1, 1, 0, 2), * k1, p2; repeat from *, end k1, p0 (1, 1, 2, 0). Repeat round 1 until neckband measures 1". Bind off in rib. Sew top of sleeves to straight edges of armholes. Sew straight portion at top of sleeves to bound-off armhole stitches. Sew side and sleeve seams.

Chart A

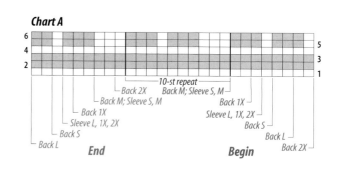

6
4
2
5
3
1

10-st repeat
Back 2X   Back M; Sleeve S, M
Back M; Sleeve S, M   Back 1X
Back 1X   Sleeve L, 1X, 2X
Sleeve L, 1X, 2X   Back S
Back S   Back L
Back L   Back 2X
End   **Begin**

Chart B

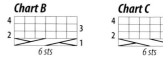

4   3
2   1
6 sts

Chart C

4   3
2   1
6 sts

Stitch key

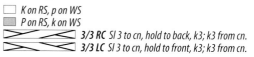

☐ K on RS, p on WS
▨ P on RS, k on WS
✕ **3/3 RC** *Sl 3 to cn, hold to back, k3; k3 from cn.*
✕ **3/3 LC** *Sl 3 to cn, hold to front, k3; k3 from cn.*

Vests

The luxury of pure alpaca in a beautiful shade of blue will make this vest a mainstay in any man's wardrobe. A mitered V-neck easily accommodates a shirt and tie—under a blazer or not.

Julie Gaddy

Perfectly Plain Vest

EASY +

STANDARD FIT

Shown in Medium
Sizes S (M, L, 1X, 2X)
A 40½ (44, 47½, 52, 56½)"
B 24 (25, 26, 28, 28)"

10cm/4"

29

22

• over stockinette stitch (knit on RS, purl on WS), using larger needles

1 2 **3** 4 5 6

• **Light weight**
• 750 (800, 900, 1050, 1200) yds

• 3.5mm/US 4 and 4mm/US 6, or size to obtain gauge

• 3.25mm/US 3, 60cm/24" long

&

• stitch holder
• stitch markers

original yarn
RUSSI SALES Heirloom Alpaca 8 ply (alpaca; 50g; 100 yds) in Blue

Note
See *School*, page 82, for SSK.

Back
With smaller needles, cast on 111 (121, 131, 143, 155) stitches. Work in k1, p1 rib for 2½", end with a WS row. Change to larger needles. Work in stockinette stitch until piece measures 14 (14½, 15, 16, 16)" from beginning, end with a WS row.
Shape armholes
Bind off 11 (13, 15, 17, 19) stitches at beginning of next 2 rows. **Decrease row** (RS) K2, k2tog, knit to last 4 stitches, SSK, k2. Repeat Decrease row every other row 5 (5, 5, 6, 6) times more—77 (83, 89, 95, 103) stitches. Work even until armhole measures 10 (10½, 11, 12, 12)". Bind off.

Front
Work as for back until piece measures same length as back to underarm, end with a WS row.
Shape armholes and V-neck
Bind off 11 (13, 15, 17, 19) stitches at beginning of next 2 rows—89 (95, 101, 109, 117) stitches. **Decrease row** (RS) K2, k2tog, k36 (39, 42, 46, 50), SSK, k2, place next stitch on hold, join 2nd ball of yarn, k2, k2tog, knit to last 4 stitches, SSK, k2. Working both sides at same time, continue to shape armholes as for back, AT SAME TIME, continue to decrease 1 stitch at each neck edge every 4th row 13 (14, 15, 14, 17) times more, then every 6th row 2 (2, 2, 4, 2) times—22 (24, 26, 28, 31) stitches each side. Work even until front armhole is 2 rows longer than back to shoulders. Bind off.

Finishing
Block pieces. Sew shoulder and side seams.
Neckband
With RS facing and circular needle, begin at left shoulder and pick up and knit 70 (74, 78, 84, 84) stitches evenly along left front neck, place marker (pm), knit center stitch from holder, pm, pick up and knit 70 (74, 78, 84, 84) stitches along right front neck, and 33 (35, 37, 39, 41) stitches along back neck—174 (184, 194, 208, 210) stitches. Pm, join and work in rounds as follows: *Round 1* * K1, p1; repeat from * to 2 stitches before marker, SSK, slip marker (sm), k1, sm, k2tog, p1, * k1, p1; repeat from * to end. Continue in rib pattern as established, working decreases before and after markers every round, until neckband measures ¾". Bind off all stitches in pattern, working decreases before binding off.
Armhole bands
With RS facing and circular needle, begin at underarm and pick up and knit 162 (174, 186, 210, 214) stitches evenly around armhole edge. Pm, join and work in rounds of k1, p1 rib for ¾". Bind off all stitches in pattern.

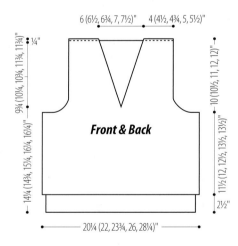

6 (6½, 6¾, 7, 7½)"   4 (4½, 4¾, 5, 5½)"

¼"

9¾ (10¼, 10¾, 11¾, 11¾)"

Front & Back

10 (10½, 11, 12, 12)"

14¼ (14¾, 15¼, 16¼, 16¼)"

11½ (12, 12½, 13½, 13½)"

2½"

20¼ (22, 23¾, 26, 28¼)"

Lois Young

Stockinette and mistake-stitch ribs lengthen the look of this vest. Color bands keep it interesting.

Basil

EASY +

STANDARD FIT

Shown in Medium
S (M, L, 1X, 2X)

A 41 (44, 47½, 51, 54½)"
B 25 (25½, 26, 26½, 26½)"

10cm/4"

24

19

• over Chart Pattern, using larger needles

1 2 3 **4** 5 6

• *Medium weight*
MC • 800 (900, 1000, 1150, 1200) yds
A • 150 yds all sizes
B • 75 yds all sizes

• 3.75mm/US 5 and 4.5mm/US 7,
or size to obtain gauge

• 3.75mm/US 5, 40cm/16" long

• stitch marker

original yarn

CASCADE 220 (wool; 100g; 220 yds)
in Green (MC), Gold (A), and Rust (B)

Back

With smaller needles and MC, cast on 97 (105, 113, 121, 129) stitches. Work Chart Pattern for 6 rows. Continue in chart pattern as follows: work 2 rows A, 2 rows B, 2 rows A, 6 rows MC. Change to larger needles. Continue in pattern with MC only until piece measures 15" from beginning, end with a WS row.
Shape armholes
Bind off 6 (7, 8, 9, 10) stitches at beginning of next 2 rows. Decrease 1 stitch each side every RS row 2 (2, 2, 3, 3) times—81 (87, 93, 97, 103) stitches. Work even until armhole measures 9 (9½, 10, 10½, 10½)", end with a WS row.
Shape shoulders
Bind off 8 (9, 10, 10, 11) stitches at beginning of next 4 rows, 8 (8, 9, 10, 10) stitches at beginning of next 2 rows. Bind off remaining 33 (35, 35, 37, 39) stitches.

Front

Work as for back to underarm.
Shape armholes
Shape armholes as for back, AT SAME TIME, work in stripe pattern as follows: 0 (4, 6, 10, 10) rows MC, [2 rows A, 2 rows MC] twice, [2 rows A, 2 rows B] 5 times, 2 rows A, 2 rows MC—81 (87, 93, 97, 103) stitches. Armhole measures approximately 5½ (6, 6½, 7, 7)".
Shape neck and shoulders
Next row (RS) With A, work 33 (35, 38, 39, 41) stitches, join 2nd ball of yarn and bind off center 15 (17, 17, 19, 21) stitches, work to end. Working both sides at same time, work as follows: Work 1 row even with A. Work 2 rows with MC, decreasing 1 stitch at each neck edge on first (RS) row. Work 2 rows with A, decreasing 1 stitch at each neck edge on first (RS) row. Continue with MC, decreasing 1 stitch at each neck edge every RS row 7 times more—24 (26, 29, 30, 32) stitches each side. Work even until armhole measures same length as back to shoulders. Shape shoulders as for back.

Finishing

Block pieces. Sew shoulders.
Neckband
With RS facing, circular needle and MC, begin at left shoulder and pick up and knit 21 stitches evenly along left front neck edge, 15 (17, 17, 19, 21) stitches along center front neck, 21 stitches along right neck edge, and 33 (35, 35, 37, 39) stitches along back neck—90 (94, 94, 98, 102) stitches. Place marker, join and [purl 1 round, knit 1 round] 3 times. Bind off purlwise. Sew side seams.
Armhole bands
Work as for neckband, picking up 100 (108, 116, 126, 128) stitches evenly around armhole.

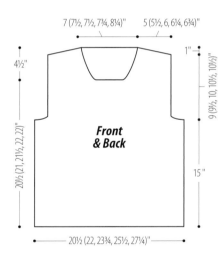

7 (7½, 7½, 7¾, 8¼)"   5 (5½, 6, 6¼, 6¾)"

4½"

9 (9½, 10, 10½, 10½)"

1"

20½ (21, 21½, 22, 22)"

Front & Back

15"

20½ (22, 23¾, 25½, 27¼)"

Chart Pattern

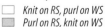

2

1

8-st repeat

Stitch key

☐ Knit on RS, purl on WS
▨ Purl on RS, knit on WS

Kathy Cheifetz

This vest is a man's clothing dream come true. Classically styled with side increases, a V-neck, and deep armholes for unrestricted movement, it gently conforms to his body. Kathy writes, "My husband's business travel often spans several climates, which creates a wardrobe crisis every time he packs for a trip. He requested the perfect travel garment that won't wrinkle, can be dressed up or down, and looks great on him. My attempts to meet the challenge have formed quite a stack of vests in his closet. It is this one, though, that he invariably puts in his suitcase. We call it his 'traveler's vest."

On The Go

INTERMEDIATE

STANDARD FIT

Shown in Extra Large
Sizes S (M, L, 1X, 2X)
A 38½ (41½, 46, 49, 53½)"
B 23½ (24, 25, 25, 26)"

10cm/4"

27

21
• **over Chart Pattern, using larger needles**

1 2 3 **4** 5 6

• **Medium weight**
• 750 (800, 950, 1100, 1250) yds

• 4mm/US 6 and 5mm/US 8,
or size to obtain gauge

• 4mm/US 6, 74cm/29" long

&

• stitch holders
• stitch marker

original yarn
JCA Jazz (wool, alpaca; 150g; 246 yds)
in Brown

Note
See *School*, page 82, for S2KP2 and 3-needle bind-off.

Back
With smaller needles, cast on 89 (97, 109, 117, 129) stitches. Work in k1, p1 rib for 2", end with a WS row. Change to larger needles. Work in Chart Pattern, increasing 1 stitch each side (working increases into pattern) on 13th row, then every 12th row 5 (5, 3, 3, 0) times, every 14th row 0 (0, 2, 2, 5) times—101 (109, 121, 129, 141) stitches. Work even until piece measures 14 (14, 14½, 14½, 15)" from beginning, end with a WS row.

Shape armholes
Bind off 4 (4, 6, 6, 7) stitches at beginning of next 2 rows. Decrease 1 stitch each side every row 10 (12, 14, 16, 18) times—73 (77, 81, 85, 91) stitches. Work even until armhole measures 9½ (10, 10½, 10½, 11)". Place stitches on hold.

Front
Work as for back until piece measures same length as back to underarm, end with a WS row.

Shape armholes and V-neck
Next row (RS) Bind off 4 (4, 6, 6, 7) stitches, work until there are 46 (50, 54, 58, 63) stitches on right needle, place center stitch on hold, join 2nd ball of yarn, work to end. Continue to shape armholes at each side as for back, AT SAME TIME, decrease 1 stitch at each neck edge every other row 7 (7, 9, 13, 13) times, then every 4th row 11 (12, 12, 10, 10) times—18 (19, 19, 19, 22) stitches each side. Work even until armhole measures same length as back to shoulders. Place stitches on hold.

Finishing
Block pieces. Join 18 (19, 19, 19, 22) stitches each side for shoulders, using 3-needle bind-off. Leave center 37 (39, 43, 47, 47) stitches on hold for back neck.
Neckband
With RS facing and circular needle, begin at left shoulder and pick up and knit 45 (49, 53, 55, 57) stitches evenly along left front neck, k1 from front neck holder (mark this stitch), pick up and knit 45 (49, 53, 55, 57) stitches along right front neck, knit 37 (39, 43, 47, 47) stitches from back neck holder and decrease 6 stitches evenly across—122 (132, 144, 152, 156) stitches. Place marker, join and work in rounds as follows: *Round 1* * K1, p1; repeat from * to 1 stitch before marked stitch, work S2KP2 over next 3 stitches, * p1, k1; repeat from *, end p1. *Round 2* Rib to 1 stitch before marked stitch, S2KP2, rib to end. *Rounds 3–6* Repeat round 2. Bind off all stitches, working S2KP2 at center of V before binding off.
Armhole bands
With RS facing and smaller needles, pick up and knit 105 (113, 125, 129, 139) stitches evenly around armhole edge. Work in k1, p1 rib for 5 rows. Bind off. Sew side seams, including armhole bands.

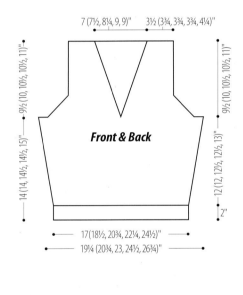

7 (7½, 8¼, 9, 9)"   3½ (3¾, 3¾, 3¾, 4¼)"

9½ (10, 10½, 10½, 11)"

Front & Back

14 (14, 14½, 14½, 15)"

9½ (10, 10½, 10½, 11)"

12 (12, 12½, 12½, 13)"

2"

17 (18½, 20¾, 22¼, 24½)"
19¼ (20¾, 23, 24½, 26¾)"

Chart Pattern

2 ← → 1
└─ 4-st repeat ─┘

Stitch key
☐ *Knit on RS, purl on WS*
▨ *Purl on RS, knit on WS*

Diane Zangl

This classic vest features an allover pattern of Bavarian twist stitches adapted patterns from Maria Erlbacher's Bäuerliches Stricken. The designs flow into the armhole and neckline where decreases are worked inside the 2-stitch lines which separate the pattern. Remember to work all knit stitches through the back loop at all times. Since this vest is worked in the round using steeks, it is easy to see the stitches.

Herz & Baum

ADVANCED

STANDARD FIT

Shown in Large
Sizes M (L)
A 42 (46½)"
B 26¼ (26¾)"

10cm/4"

28
29
• *over Chart Patterns, using larger needles*

1 2 3 **4** 5 6

• *Medium weight*
• 1400 (1600) yds

3.25mm/US 3 and 3.75mm/US 5, 60cm (24")
long, or size to obtain gauge
3.25mm/US 3, 40cm (16") long

&

• stitch holders
• stitch markers
• cable needle (cn)

original yarn

BROWN SHEEP Lamb's Pride Superwash;
(wool; 50g; 100 yds) Misty Blue

Notes

1 See *School*, page 82, for SSK through back loop (tbl), k2tog tbl and steeks. **2** Vest is worked circularly to shoulders, with steeks at center front neck and armholes. **3** Steek stitches are not included in stitch counts or measurements. **4** Work 4 steek stitches every round as follows: k1 tbl, k2, k1 tbl.

Neck and armhole decreases

Left-slanting decrease (worked over first 4 stitches of section) P1, k1 tbl, k2tog tbl. (On rounds without decreases, work first 3 stitches as follows: P1, k2 tbl.)
Right-slanting decrease (worked over last 4 stitches of section) SSK tbl, k1 tbl, p1. (On rounds without decreases, work last 3 stitches as follows: K2 tbl, p1.)

Body

With smaller 24" needle, cast on 304 (336) stitches. Place marker (pm), join, and work in rounds as follows: *Begin Twisted Rib: Round 1* K1 tbl, * p2, k2 tbl; repeat from *, end p2, k1 tbl. Repeat Round 1 until ribbing measures 2". Change to larger needle. *Begin Chart Patterns: Foundation Rounds 1 and 2* * [K1 tbl, p2, k1 tbl, pm] 0 (1) time, work 12 stitches Chart A, pm, 16 stitches Chart C, pm, 12 stitches Chart A, pm, 14 stitches Chart D, pm, 12 (16) stitches Chart A (B), pm, 20 stitches Chart E, pm, 12 (16) stitches Chart A (B), pm, 14 stitches Chart D, pm, 12 stitches Chart A, pm, 16 stitches Chart C, pm, 12 stitches Chart A, pm, [k1 tbl, p2, k1 tbl, pm] 0 (1) time; repeat from * once more, omitting last marker placement. Continue in chart patterns as established until 26-round repeat of Chart E has been worked 3 times, then work chart rounds 1—10 once more, ending last round 10 (14) stitches before round marker. Piece measures approximately 14¾" from beginning.

Shape V-neck and armholes

Next round Bind off 20 (28) stitches (for left underarm), removing marker(s), work until there are 65 (69) stitches on right needle (for left front), work 1/1 RC (center 2 stitches of round 11 of Chart E) and place these stitches on hold, work 65 (69) stitches (for right front), bind off 20 (28) stitches (for right underarm), removing marker(s), work remaining 132 (140) stitches (for back)—262 (278) stitches.
Next round Pm (for new beginning of round), cast on 4 stitches (armhole steek), pm, p1, k2 tbl, work to 3 stitches before neck edge, 1/1 RC, p1, pm, cast on 4 stitches (neck steek), pm, p1, 1/1 LC, work to 3 stitches before right underarm, k2 tbl, p1, pm, cast on 4 stitches (armhole steek), pm, p1, k2 tbl, work to last 3 stitches of round, k2 tbl, p1. Working in patterns as established, decrease 1 stitch at each armhole edge on next round, then every other round 3 times more, AT SAME TIME, decrease 1 stitch at each neck edge every 3rd round 24 (26) times—37 (39) stitches for each front and 124 (132) stitches for back. Work even until armhole measures 11½ (12)". Bind off.

Finishing

Block piece. Secure steek stitches with crochet chain. Cut through center of steeks. Sew shoulders.

Neckband

With RS facing and smaller 24" needle, begin at left shoulder and pick up and knit 65 (69) stitches evenly along left front neck, k1 tbl from holder, pm, k1 tbl from holder, then pick up and knit 65 (69) stitches along right front neck, and 50 (54) stitches along back neck—182 (194) stitches. Pm, join, and work Twisted Rib in rounds as follows: *Round 1* [K2 tbl, p2] 16 (17) times, SSK tbl, k2tog tbl, [p2, k2 tbl] 28 (30) times, p2. *Round 2* Work rib pattern as established to 2 stitches before marker, SSK tbl, k2tog tbl, rib to end. Repeat Round 2 until neckband measures 1". Bind off in pattern.

Armhole bands

With RS facing and 16" needle, begin at center of underarm and pick up and knit 160 (168) stitches evenly around armhole edge. PM, join and work Twisted Rib in rounds as follows: *Rounds 1&2* P2, [k2tbl, p2] twice, k3tbl, p3, [k2tbl, p2] 32 (34) times, k3tbl, p3, [k2tbl, p2] twice, k2tbl. *Round 3* P2, [k2tbl, p2] twice, *k1tbl, SSK tbl, p2tog, p1*, [k2tbl, p2] 32(34) times, repeat from * to * once, [k2tbl, p2] twice, k2tbl. *Round 4* *P2, k2tbl; repeat from * to end. Repeat round 4 until armhole band measures 1". Bind off in pattern.

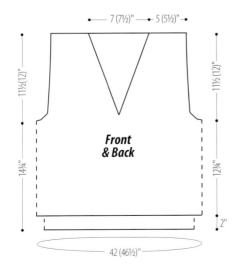

← 7 (7½)" → ← 5 (5½)" →

11½ (12)"

11½ (12)"

14¾"

12¾"

Front & Back

2"

42 (46½)"

Chart A

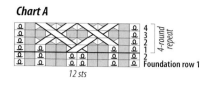

4-round repeat

4
3
2
1
Foundation row 1

12 sts

Chart B

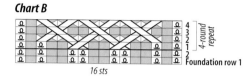

4-round repeat

4
3
2
1
Foundation row 1

16 sts

Chart C

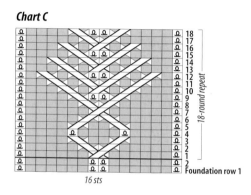

18-round repeat

18
17
16
15
14
13
12
11
10
9
8
7
6
5
4
3
2
1
Foundation row 1

16 sts

Chart D

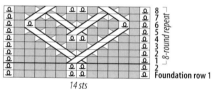

8-round repeat

8
7
6
5
4
3
2
1
Foundation row 1

14 sts

Chart E

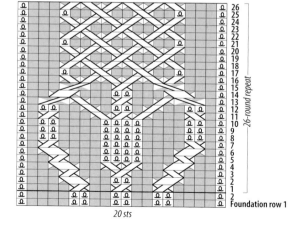

26-round repeat

26
25
24
23
22
21
20
19
18
17
16
15
14
13
12
11
10
9
8
7
6
5
4
3
2
1
Foundation row 1

20 sts

Stitch key

- Ⓤ *Knit tbl*
- ▢ *Purl*
- 1/1 RC *Sl 1 to cn, hold to back, k1 tbl; k1 tbl from cn.*
- 1/1 LC *Sl 1 to cn, hold to front, k1 tbl; k1 tbl from cn.*
- 1/1 RPC *Sl 1 to cn, hold to back, k1 tbl; p1 from cn.*
- 1/1 LPC *Sl 1 to cn, hold to front, p1; k1 tbl from cn.*
- 2/1 RPC *Sl 1 to cn, hold to back, k2 tbl; p1 from cn.*
- 2/1 LPC *Sl 2 to cn, hold to front, p1; k2 tbl from cn.*
- 1/1/1 RPC *Sl 2 to cn, hold to back; k1 tbl, sl last st from cn to left needle and k1 tbl; p1 from cn.*
- 1/1/1 LPC *Sl 2 to cn, hold to front, p1; sl last st from cn to left needle and k1 tbl; k1 tbl from cn.*

Back and Front Pattern Arrangement

K1 tbl, p2, k1 tbl (size L only)	12 sts Chart A	16 sts Chart C	12 sts Chart A	14 sts Chart D	12(16) sts ChartA(B)	20 sts Chart E	12(16) sts ChartA(B)	14 sts Chart D	12 sts Chart A	16 sts Chart C	12 sts Chart A	K1 tbl, p2, k1 tbl (size L only)

Diane Zangl

The patterning on the wings of a cecropia moth inspired this pattern. When you strand two marled yarns through the stitch pattern, it looks like an aged, printed graphic. The circular construction uses steeks, making for easy knitting and perhaps a new experience in finishing.

Cecropia

INTERMEDIATE +

B | A
LOOSE FIT

S (M/L, 1X, 2X/3X)
Shown in Small
A 40¾ (46½, 52¼, 58¼)"
B 24 (25, 25½, 26½)"

10cm/4"

24
22
• **over Chart Pattern, using larger needles**

 1 2 3 **4** 5 6

• **Medium weight**
MC • 575 (685, 785, 910) yds
CC • 430 (515, 590, 680) yds

• 3.5mm/US 4 and 3.75mm/US 5, or size to
obtain gauge, 72cm (29") long
• 3.5mm/US 4, 40cm (16") long

 &

• stitch holder
• stitch markers

original yarn

KNIT ONE, CROCHET TOO 2nd Time Cotton
(recycled cotton, acrylic; 100g; 180 yds)
Light blue (MC) and Medium blue (CC)

Notes

1 See *School*, page 82, for SSK, S2KP2, and steeks. **2** Vest is knit circularly to shoulders, with steeks at center front neck and armholes (see illustration). **3** Steek stitches are not included in stitch counts or measurements. **4** Work 4 steek stitches every round as follows: k1 through back loop (tbl), k2, k1 tbl. **5** On chart rounds with 2 colors, work steek stitches as follows: [1 MC, 1 CC] twice. **6** Carry unused color loosely across back of work to avoid puckering fabric. Where long carries of CC occur, catch yarn every 3–4 stitches to avoid long loops.

Twisted Rib Pattern *MULTIPLE OF 4 STITCHES*

Rounds 1 and 2 With MC, *[k1 tbl] twice, p2; repeat from *.
Rounds 3 and 4 With CC, repeat round 1.
Repeat Rounds 1–4 for Twisted Rib Pattern.

Body

With smaller 29" needle and MC, cast on 200 (228, 260, 288) stitches. Place marker (pm), join, and work in Twisted Rib Pattern for 10 rounds. Change to larger needle. With MC, knit 1 round, increasing 24 (28, 28, 32) stitches evenly around—224 (256, 288, 320) stitches.

Begin Chart Pattern: **Round 1** Work 16-stitch repeat of chart 7 (8, 9, 10) times, pm (for side "seam"), work 16-stitch repeat of chart to end. Continue in chart pattern as established until piece measures 13 (14, 14½, 15)" from beginning.

Shape V-neck and armholes

Next round Work 55 (63, 71, 79) stitches, k2tog and place this stitch on hold, work to end of round. **Next round** Work to neck edge, pm, cast on 4 stitches (neck steek), pm, work to end of round. **Decrease round** Work to 2 stitches before neck marker, k2tog, work steek stitches, SSK, work to end of round. Repeat decrease round every 3rd round 18 (18, 18, 19) times more, AT SAME TIME, when neck measures 2 (1, ½, ½)", end round 15 stitches before round marker, then work as follows: bind off 30 stitches for left underarm (removing marker), work to 15 stitches before side "seam" marker, bind off 30 stitches for right underarm (removing marker), work to end. **Next round** Pm (for new beginning of round) cast on 4 stitches (armhole steek), pm, work to right underarm, pm, cast on 4 stitches (armhole steek), pm, work to end of round.

Shape armholes

Decrease round Work armhole steek stitches, SSK, work to 2 stitches before next armhole marker, k2tog, work steek stitches, SSK, work to last 2 stitches, k2tog. Continue to shape V-neck and repeat armhole decrease round every other round 4 (6, 10, 13) times more—16 (22, 26, 30) stitches for each front shoulder and 72 (84, 92, 102) stitches for back. Work even until armhole measures 8 (9, 9½, 10)".

Shape front shoulders

Begin working back and forth in rows as follows: **Next row** (RS) Bind off 9 (11, 13, 14) stitches (including steek stitches), removing markers, work to next armhole

steek, work 4 steek stitches, turn. **Next row** (WS) Bind off 9 (11, 13, 14) stitches (including steek stitches), work to V-neck steek stitches, p1 tbl, p2, p1 tbl, work to end. **Next 2 rows** Bind off 5 (7, 9, 10) stitches, work to end of front. **Next row** (RS) Bind off 6 (8, 8, 10) stitches, work to end of front. **Next row** (WS) Bind off 10 (12, 12, 14) stitches (including neck steek stitches).

Shape back shoulders

With RS facing, join yarn at armhole edge and bind off 5 (7, 9, 10) stitches at beginning of next 4 rows, 6 (8, 8, 10) stitches at beginning of next 2 rows. Bind off remaining 40 (40, 40, 42) stitches.

Finishing

Block piece. Secure steek stitches with crochet chain. Cut through center of steeks. Sew shoulders.

Neckband

With RS facing, 16" circular needle, and MC, begin at left shoulder and pick up and knit 65 (65, 65, 69) stitches along left front neck, k1 from center neck holder, then pick up and knit 65 (65, 65, 69) stitches along right front neck and 38 (38, 38, 42) stitches along back neck—169 (169, 169, 181) stitches. Pm, join and work Twisted Rib Pattern in rounds as follows: **Round 1** [K2 tbl, p2] 16 (16, 16, 17) times, S2KP2, [p2, k2 tbl] 25 (25, 25, 27) times, p2. **Round 2** Work in rib pattern as established to 1 stitch before center front neck stitch, S2KP2 over center 3 stitches, work in rib pattern to end of round. **Rounds 3 and 4** With CC, repeat round 2. **Rounds 5 and 6** With MC, repeat round 2. Bind off in rib.

Armhole bands

With RS facing, 16" circular needle and MC, begin at center of underarm and pick up and knit 120 (128, 132, 136) stitches evenly around armhole edge. Pm, join and work Twisted Rib Pattern as follows: 2 rounds MC, 2 rounds CC, 2 rounds MC. Bind off in rib.

7¼ (7¼, 7¼, 7½)" 3 (4, 4¾, 5½)"
1"
11 (11, 11, 11½)"
8 (9, 9½, 10)"
13 (14, 14½, 15)"
13½ (13½, 13½, 14)"
Front & Back
1½"
40¾ (46½, 52¼, 58¼)"

Chart Pattern

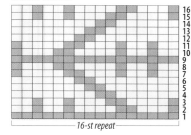

16-st repeat

Stitch key

☐ Knit (rounds)
Knit on RS, purl on WS (rows)

Color key

☐ MC
▨ CC

Steeks shown in blue.

8 needle

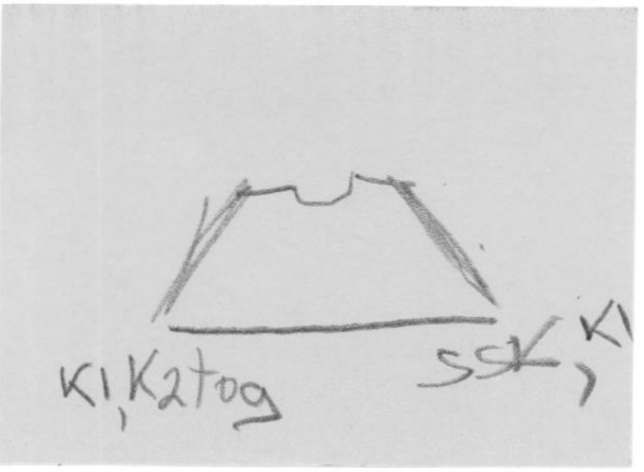

K1, K2tog
SSK, K1

Silhouette and color combine for a ves
tattersall check is easy to knit: horizont
later. This vest uses the traditional color placement and classic Fair Isle borders.

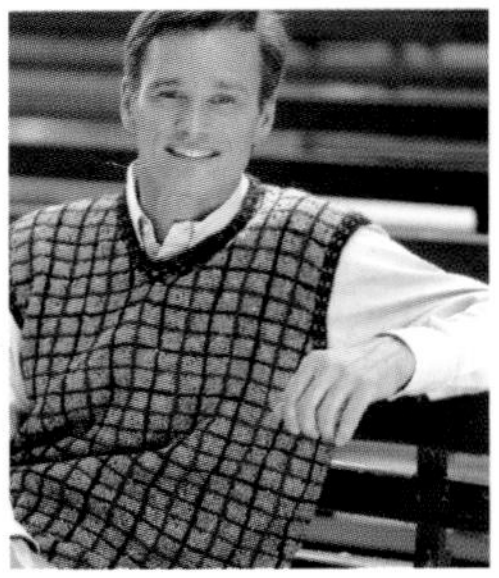

Nancy Marchant

Crossed Lines

INTERMEDIATE

B A

LOOSE FIT

Shown in Large

Sizes M (L, 1X, 2X)

A 43 (47½, 52½, 57)"

B 24¼ (25¼, 27, 28)"

10cm/4"

25

20

• over Chart B, using larger needles

1 2 **3** 4 5 6

• Light weight

MC • 700 (800, 950, 1100) yds

A & B • 225 (250, 300, 350) yds each

• 4mm/US 6, or size to obtain gauge

• 3.5mm/US 4, 40cm (16") long

• 4mm/G/6

&

• stitch holders

• stitch markers

original yarn

SR KERTZER Naturally Tussock DK (wool, polyester; 100g; 203 yds) in Gray (MC), Red (A) and Blue (B)

Note

For Chart B, work vertical stripes along columns of purl stitches after pieces are complete, using slip stitch crochet (see illustrations on opposite page), and alternating A and B stripes.

Back

With larger needles and A, cast on 101 (113, 125, 137) stitches. Work 10 rows of Chart A. *Next row* (RS) With MC, knit and increase 6 stitches evenly across—107 (119, 131, 143) stitches. Beginning with a WS row, work Chart B until piece measures 14½ (15½, 16¼, 17¼)" above turning ridge, end with a WS row.

Shape armholes

Bind off 9 stitches at beginning of next 2 rows. Decrease 1 stitch each side on next row, then every other row 7 times more—73 (85, 97, 109) stitches. Work even until armhole measures 9¼ (9¼, 10¼, 10¼)", end with a WS row.

Shape shoulders

Bind off 10 (13, 15, 18) stitches at beginning of next 4 rows. Bind off remaining 33 (33, 37, 37) stitches.

Front

Work as for back until armhole measures 3½", end with a WS row.

Shape V-neck

Next row (RS) Work 36 (42, 48, 54) stitches, place center stitch on hold, join 2nd ball of yarn and work to end. Working both sides at same time, decrease 1 stitch at each neck edge every other row 16 (16, 18, 18) times—20 (26, 30, 36) stitches each side. Work even until armhole measures same length as back to shoulders. Shape shoulders as for back.

Finishing

Block pieces. Work slip stitch crochet vertical stripes on front and back. Sew shoulder and side seams. Fold lower edge band to WS at turning ridge and sew in place.

Neckband

With RS facing, circular needle and B, begin at right shoulder and pick up and knit 33 (33, 36, 36) stitches evenly along back neck, 31 (31, 37, 37) stitches along left front neck, k1 from center front holder (mark this stitch), pick up and knit 31 (31, 37, 37) stitches along right front neck—96 (96, 111, 111) stitches. Place marker (pm), join and work in rounds as follows: *Begin Chart C: Round 1* Work 3-stitch repeat of chart 20 (20, 23, 23) times, work last 9 stitches of chart (marked stitch on chart should fall at marked center front stitch of V), then work 3-stitch repeat of chart 9 (9, 11, 11) times. Continue in pattern as established through chart round 9. Fold neckband to WS at turning ridge and sew in place.

Armhole bands

With RS facing, circular needle and B, begin at underarm and pick up and knit 99 (99, 105, 105) stitches evenly around armhole edge. Pm, join and, working 3-stitch repeat only, work 9 rounds of Chart C. Fold band at turning ridge and sew in place.

Chart A

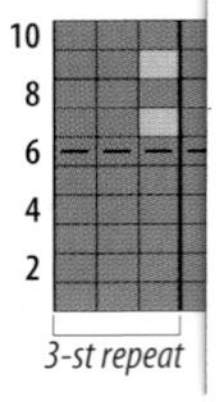

10
8
6
4
2
3-st repeat

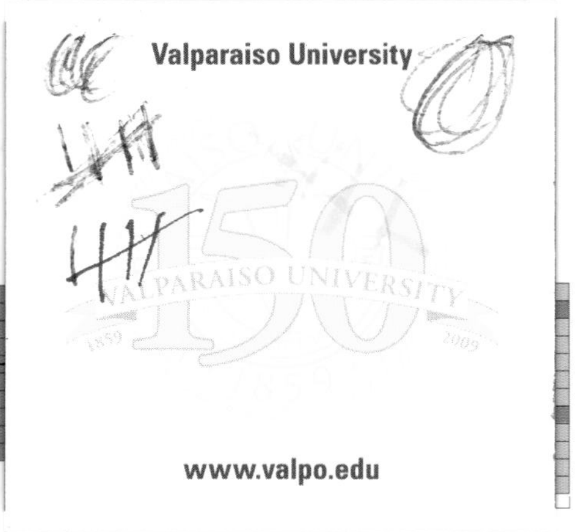

Valparaiso University
150
VALPARAISO UNIVERSITY
www.valpo.edu

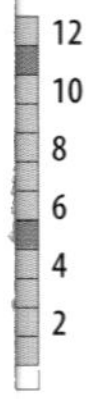

12
10
8
6
4
2

Note: *For Chart B, work slip stitch crochet vertical stripes (alternating A & B) along vertical columns of purl stitches after piece is complete.*

Chart C

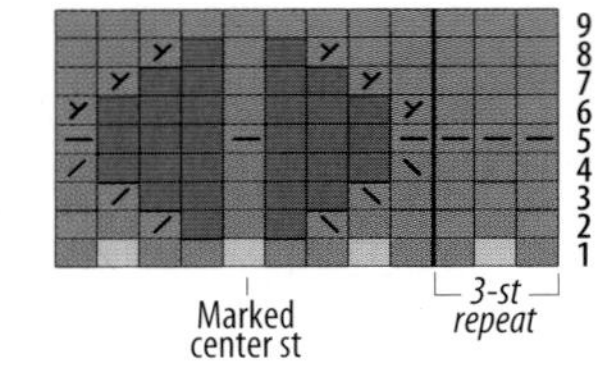

9
8
7
6
5
4
3
2
1
Marked center st
3-st repeat

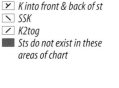

Stitch key

- K on RS, p on WS
- P on RS, k on WS
- K into front & back of st
- SSK
- K2tog
- Sts do not exist in these areas of chart

Color key

- MC
- A
- B

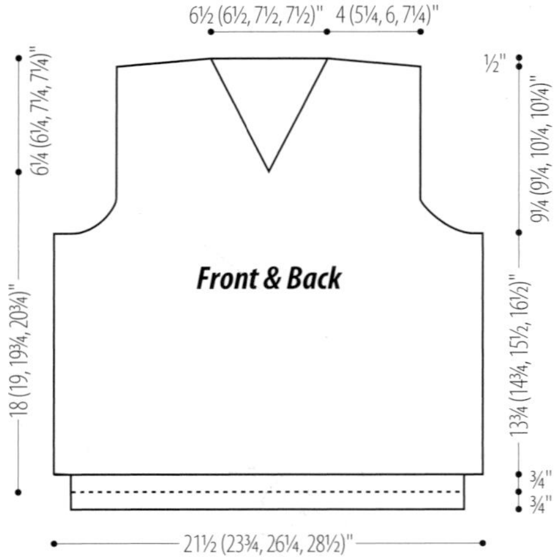

6½ (6½, 7½, 7½)"
4 (5¼, 6, 7¼)"
½"
6¼ (6¼, 7¼, 7¼)"
9¼ (9¼, 10¼, 10¼)"
Front & Back
18 (19, 19¾, 20¾)"
13¾ (14¾, 15½, 16½)"
¾"
¾"
21½ (23¾, 26¼, 28½)"

SLIP STITCH CROCHET VERTICAL STRIPES

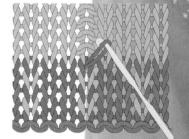

1 Insert crochet hook into last B row at bottom of vertical column of purl stitches and pull up a loop of A or B.

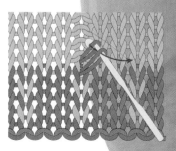

2 Insert hook into next stitch up and pull a loop through stitch and loop on hook. Repeat Step 2 until vertical stripe is complete.

This vest was inspired by a basketweave pattern from a mans sock. The knit panels appear to stand out on the purl background, creating the illusion of vertical lines. The design is versatile enough to please both the 'man-about-town' and the 'country gentleman'.

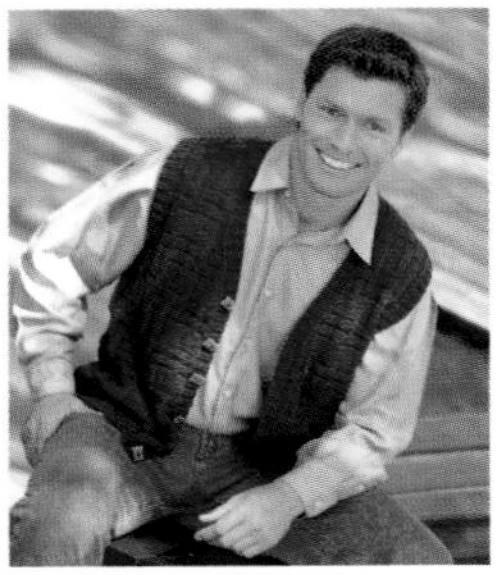

Kathy Zimmerman

Basketweave Green

INTERMEDIATE

B A

STANDARD FIT

Shown in Medium

Sizes S (M, L, 1X, 2X, 3X)

A 40½ (42¾, 45¼, 50, 54½, 57)"

B 24 (25, 25½, 26, 26½, 26½)"

10cm/4"

31

22

• over Chart Pattern, using larger needles

1 2 3 **4** 5 6

• Medium weight

• 825 (900, 1000, 1100, 1200, 1250) yds

• 3.75mm/US 5 and 4.5mm/US 7, or size to obtain gauge, 74cm/29" long

• 3.75mm/US 5, 40cm/16" long

• 5 (6, 6, 6, 6, 6) 25mm/1"

&

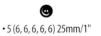

• stitch holders

• stitch markers

original yarn

SPINRITE Muskoka Worsted Weight (wool; 100g; 200yds) Green

Notes

1 See *School*, page 82, for 3-row buttonhole. **2** Body is worked in one piece to underarm, then divided for fronts and back.

Body

With smaller 29" needle, cast on 200 (212, 224, 248, 272, 284) stitches. ***Begin Rib Pattern: Row 1*** (RS) K1, p2, * k2, p2; repeat from *, end k1. ***Row 2*** P1, k2, * p2, k2; repeat from *, end p1. Repeat Rows 1 and 2 until rib measures 1½", increasing 17 (18, 19, 21, 23, 24) stitches evenly across last row—217 (230, 243, 269, 295, 308) stitches. Change to larger needle. Work in Chart Pattern until piece measures 14 (14½, 15, 15½, 15½, 15½)" from beginning, end with a WS row.

Divide for fronts and back

Next row (RS) Work 48 (50, 53, 58, 62, 64) stitches (for right front), bind off 11 (13, 15, 19, 23, 25) stitches (for underarm), work until there are 99 (104, 107, 115, 125, 130) stitches on right needle (for back), bind off 11 (13, 15, 19, 23, 25) stitches (for underarm), work to end (for left front). ***Next row*** (WS) Work 48 (50, 53, 58, 62, 64) stitches of left front and place remaining stitches on hold.

Left Front

Shape armhole and V-neck

At beginning of every RS row (armhole edge), bind off 2 stitches 3 times, then decrease 1 stitch 5 (5, 5, 7, 9, 9) times, AT SAME TIME, decrease 1 stitch at neck edge (end of RS rows) on next row, then every other row 0 (0, 1, 5, 3, 3) times more, every 4th row 12 (13, 17, 15, 17, 17) times, every 6th row 3 (3, 0, 0, 0, 0) times—21 (22, 23, 24, 26, 28) stitches. Work 1 row even. Armhole measures approximately 9 (9½, 9½, 9½, 10, 10)".

Shape shoulder

Bind off at armhole edge 5 (5, 5, 6, 6, 7) stitches 3 (2, 1, 4, 2, 4) times, 6 (6, 6, 0, 7, 0) stitches 1 (2, 3, 0, 2, 0) times.

Right Front

With WS facing, join yarn and work to correspond to left front, reversing shaping. Shape armhole by working bind-offs at begging of WS rows and decreases at end of RS rows. Shape V-neck by working decreases at beginning of RS rows. Shape shoulder by working bind-offs at beginning of WS rows.

Back

With WS facing, join yarn and shape armholes as for fronts—77 (82, 85, 89, 95, 100) stitches. Work even until armhole measures same length as fronts to shoulder shaping. Mark center 27 (30, 31, 33, 35, 36) stitches.

Shape shoulders and neck

Shape shoulders as for fronts, AT SAME TIME, join a 2nd ball of yarn and bind off marked stitches and, working both sides at same time, bind off from each neck edge 2 stitches once, 1 stitch twice.

Finishing

Block pieces. Sew shoulders.

Front bands

Place markers (pm) along left front for 5 (6, 6, 6, 6, 6) buttonholes, with the first ½" below beginning of V-neck shaping, the last ½" above lower edge, and 3 (4, 4, 4, 4, 4) others spaced evenly between. With RS facing and smaller 29" needle, pick up and knit 82 (85, 88, 91, 91, 91) stitches evenly along right front edge to beginning of V-neck shaping, 1 stitch at first neck decrease (mark this stitch), 63 (65, 65, 68, 72, 72) stitches to shoulder, 38 (40, 42, 42, 46, 46) stitches along back neck, 63 (65, 65, 68, 72, 72) stitches to beginning of left front V-neck shaping, 1 stitch at first neck decrease (mark this stitch) and 82 (85, 88, 91, 91, 91) stitches to lower edge—330 (342, 350, 362, 374, 374) stitches. ***Begin Rib Pattern: Row 1*** (WS) P2, * k2, p2; repeat from * to end, increasing 1 stitch each side of each marked stitch at front V-neck (working increases into rib pattern)—334 (346, 354, 366, 378, 378) stitches. ***Rows 2–7*** Work in rib pattern as established, working 3-row buttonholes on left front at markers on rows 3-5. Bind off.

Armhole bands

With RS facing and 16" needle, pick up and knit 128 (136, 140, 148, 160, 164) stitches evenly around armhole edge. Pm, join, and work in k2, p2 rib for 7 rounds. Bind off. Sew on buttons.

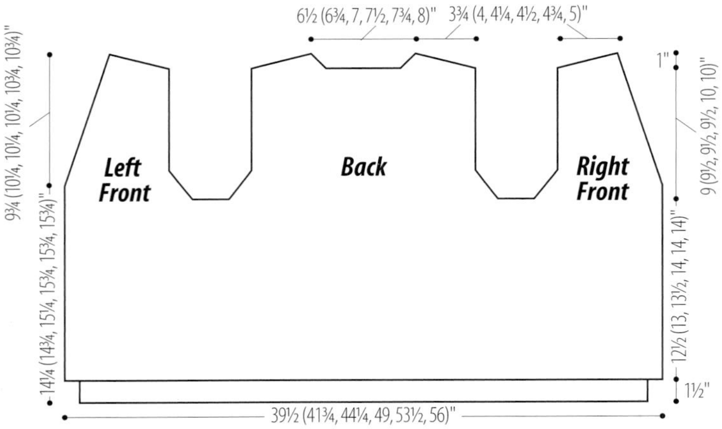
6½ (6¾, 7, 7½, 7¾, 8)"
3¾ (4, 4¼, 4½, 4¾, 5)"
1"
9¾ (10¼, 10¼, 10¼, 10¾, 10¾)"
9 (9½, 9½, 9½, 10, 10)"
Left Front
Back
Right Front
14¼ (14¾, 15¼, 15¾, 15¾, 15¾)"
12½ (13, 13½, 14, 14, 14)"
1½"
39½ (41¾, 44¼, 49, 53½, 56)"

Chart Pattern

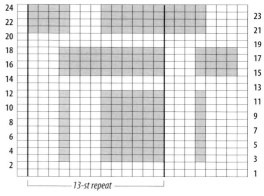

13-st repeat

Color key

☐ Knit on RS, purl on WS
▨ Purl on RS, knit on WS

Kathy Zimmerman

Here's the ultimate working vest. Real estate or construction? Banking or finance?
Customize the motifs to your own (or some other lucky person's) occupation.
For more choices, see page 80.

What's My Line

INTERMEDIATE

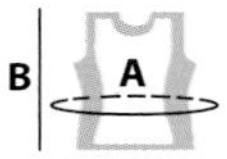

B | **A**

LOOSE FIT

Shown in Medium
Sizes XS (S, M, L, 1X, 2X)
A 37¾ (41, 44¼, 47½, 50¾, 54¼)"
B 23 (24, 24¼, 25, 25, 25)"

10cm/4"

24

22
• **over Chart A or B, using larger needles**

1 2 3 4 5 6

• **Medium weight**
MC 575 (650, 700, 775, 850, 900)
A 100 (125, 150, 175, 200, 225)
B,C 125 (150, 175, 200, 225, 250)

3.75mm/US 5 and 4mm/US 6,
or size to obtain gauge, 74cm (29") long
3.75mm/US 5 40cm (16") long

6 (6, 7, 7, 7, 7) 20mm/¾"

&

• stitch holders
• stitch markers

original yarn

CLASSIC ELITE Tapestry (wool, mohair; 50g; 95 yds)
Dollars and Cents vest: Scrolled Olive (MC),
Ibex (A), Maroon (B) and Gobelin Green (C).
House vest: Navy (MC), Madder (A), Ibex (B)
and Rug Red (C).

Notes

1 See *School*, page 82, for SSK. **2** Vest is worked in one piece to underarm, then divided for fronts and back.

DECREASE ROWS

At beginning of RS rows K1, SSK.
At end of RS rows K2tog, k1.

Vest

With smaller 29" needle and MC, cast on 200 (218, 236, 254, 272, 290) stitches.
Begin Pinstripe Rib: Rows 1 and 3 (WS) With MC, knit. *Row 2* Knit. *Rows 4 and 6* P2MC, *k1A, p2MC; repeat from *. *Rows 5 and 7* K2MC, *p1A, k2MC; repeat from *. *Rows 8-10* With MC, knit. *Row 11* Knit, increasing 1 stitch—201 (219, 237, 255, 273, 291) stitches. Change to larger needle. Work Chart A or B until piece measures 13 (13.5, 14, 14, 14, 14)" from beginning, end with a WS row.
Divide for fronts and back
Next row (RS) Work 41 (44, 47, 50, 55, 58) stitches (for right front), bind off 16 (19, 22, 25, 24, 26) stitches (for underarm), work until there are 87 (93, 99, 105, 115, 123) stitches for back, bind off 16 (19, 22, 25, 24, 26) stitches (for underarm), work to end (for left front). *Next row* (WS) Work 41 (44, 47, 50, 55, 58) stitches of left front and place remaining stitches on hold.

Left Front

Shape armhole and V-neck
Next row (RS) Bind off 2 stitches (armhole edge), work to last 3 stitches, k2tog, k1 (neck edge). Continue to bind off at armhole edge at beginning of every RS row 2 stitches 0 (0, 1, 1, 2, 3) times, then decrease 1 stitch 6 (7, 6, 7, 8, 8) times, AT SAME TIME, continue to decrease 1 stitch at neck edge every other row 5 times, then every 4th row 9 (10, 10, 11, 11, 11) times—18 (19, 21, 22, 24, 25) stitches. Work even until armhole measures 9 (9.5, 9.5, 10, 10, 10)", end with a WS row.
Shape shoulder
Bind off from armhole edge 6 (6, 7, 7, 8, 8) stitches twice, then 6 (7, 7, 8, 8, 9) stitches once.

Right Front

With WS facing, join yarn and work to correspond to left front, reversing shaping. Work armhole bind-offs at beginning of WS rows and decreases at end of RS rows. Work neck decreases at beginning of RS rows. Shape shoulders at beginning of WS rows.

Back

With WS facing, join yarn and shape armholes as for fronts—71 (75, 79, 83, 87, 91) stitches. Work even until armhole measures same length as fronts to shoulder shaping. Mark center 31 (33, 33, 35, 35, 37) stitches.

Shape shoulders and neck
Bind off 6 (6, 7, 7, 8, 8) stitches at beginning of next 4 rows, 6 (7, 7, 8, 8, 9) stitches at beginning of next 2 rows, AT SAME TIME, join 2nd ball of yarn and bind off center marked stitches for neck and, working both sides at same time, decrease 1 stitch at each neck edge every other row twice.

Finishing

Block piece. Sew shoulders. Place markers for 6 (6, 7, 7, 7, 7) buttonholes evenly along left front, with the first at beginning of V-neck shaping, the last ½" from lower edge, and 4 (4, 5, 5, 5, 5) others spaced evenly between.
Front and neckband
With RS facing, smaller 29" needle and MC, begin at lower edge and pick up and knit 58 (62, 65, 65, 65, 65) stitches evenly along right front edge to beginning of V-neck shaping, 59 (63, 63, 68, 68, 68) stitches to shoulder seam, 41 (43, 43, 45, 45, 48) stitches along back neck, 59 (63, 63, 68, 68, 68) stitches along left front neck to beginning of V-neck shaping, and 58 (62, 65, 65, 65, 65) stitches to lower edge—275 (293, 299, 311, 311, 314) stitches. Work rows 3-10 of Pinstripe Rib, working buttonholes (yo twice, k2tog) at markers on row 6. On row 7, knit into double yo, dropping wraps. When band is complete, bind off knitwise with MC on WS.
Armhole bands
With RS facing, 16" needle and MC, begin at center of underarm and pick up and knit 126 (132, 135, 141, 147, 150) stitches evenly around armhole edge. Place marker, join, and work Pinstripe Rib in rounds as follows: *Round 1* With MC, purl. *Rounds 2-5* *P2MC, k1A; repeat from *. *Rounds 6 and 8* With MC, knit. *Round 7* With MC, purl. Bind off purlwise with MC. Sew on buttons.

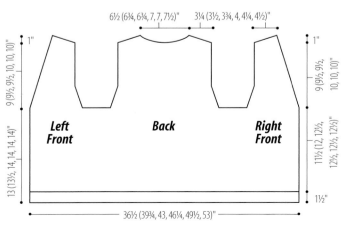

6½ (6¾, 6¾, 7, 7, 7½)"   3¼ (3½, 3¾, 4, 4¼, 4½)"

1"   1"

9 (9½, 9½, 10, 10, 10)"

9 (9½, 9½, 10, 10, 10)"

Left Front   **Back**   **Right Front**

13 (13½, 14, 14, 14, 14)"

11½ (12, 12½, 12½, 12½, 12½)"

1½"

36½ (39¾, 43, 46¼, 49½, 53)"

Chart A

24
20
10
1

— 6-st repeat —

Stitch key

☐ Knit on RS, purl on WS

Color key
■ MC
■ A
■ B
■ C

Chart B

28
20
10
1

— 18-st repeat —

Color key
■ MC
■ A
■ B
■ C

Knitter's Design Team

Handsome as a game show host and ready for action; wear this vest under a jacket or as the top layer on casual Friday. You can't miss with the color combination of black and brown heather.

Bachelor #1

INTERMEDIATE

CLOSE FIT

Shown in Medium
S (M, L, 1X, 2X)
A 37½ (40½, 43¾, 46¾, 50¼)"
B 23 (23, 24½, 25, 26)"

10cm/4"

20
over Chart Pattern, using larger needles

1 2 **3** 4 5 6

• **Light weight**
MC • 525 (575, 675, 750, 825) yds
CC • 500 (550, 625, 675, 750) yds

• 4.5mm/US 7, or size to obtain gauge

• 4mm/US 6, 40cm (16") and 80cm (32") long

• five 13mm/½"

&

• stitch holders
• stitch markers

original yarn

JO SHARP Classic DK Wool (wool; 50g; 107 yds)
Black (MC) and Brown (CC)

Note

See *School*, page 82, for 3-needle bind-off.

Back

With larger needles and MC, cast on 82 (90, 98, 106, 114) stitches. Knit 10 rows, increasing 9 stitches evenly across last (WS) row—91 (99, 107, 115, 123) stitches. Work Chart for Back until piece measures approximately 14½ (14½, 16, 16, 16)" from beginning, end with chart row 4.

Shape armholes

Bind off 4 (6, 8, 12, 12) stitches at beginning of next 2 rows. Decrease 1 stitch each side every RS row 4 (4, 6, 6, 8) times—75 (79, 79, 79, 83) stitches. Work even until armhole measures approximately 8½ (8½, 8½, 9, 10)", end with chart row 4. Place stitches on hold.

Left Front

With MC, cast on 42 (46, 50, 54, 58) stitches. Knit 10 rows, increasing 4 stitches evenly across last (WS) row—46 (50, 54, 58, 62) stitches. Work Chart for Left Front until piece measures same length as back to underarm.

Shape armhole and V-neck

Shape armhole at beginning of RS rows as for back, AT SAME TIME, decrease 1 stitch at end of next (RS) row (neck edge), then every 4th row 14 (14, 14, 14, 16) times more—23 (25, 25, 25, 25) stitches. Work even until armhole measures same length as back. Place stitches on hold.

Right Front

Work to correspond to left front, working Chart for Right Front and reversing shaping. Reverse armhole shaping by working bind-off at beginning of a WS row and decreases at end of RS rows. Work neck decreases at beginning of RS rows.

Finishing

Block pieces. With MC, join shoulders, using 3-needle bind-off, as follows: Join 23 (25, 25, 25, 25) stitches of first shoulder, bind off back neck stitches until 23 (25, 25, 25, 25) stitches remain, join 2nd shoulder.

Front and neckband

Place markers for 5 buttonholes along left front edge, with the first ½" from lower edge, the last at first neck decrease, and 3 others spaced evenly between. With RS facing, 32" circular needle and MC, pick up and knit 79 (79, 83, 83, 83) stitches evenly along right front to first neck decrease, 55 (55, 55, 57, 63) stitches to shoulder, 29 (29, 29, 29, 33) stitches along back neck, 55 (55, 55, 57, 63) stitches along left front neck to first neck decrease, and 79 (79, 83, 83, 83) stitches to lower edge—297 (297, 305, 309, 325) stitches. *Next row* (WS) Knit, working buttonholes (yo, k2tog) at left front markers. Knit 7 rows more. Bind off.

Armhole bands

With RS facing, 16" circular needle and MC, pick up and knit 96 (100, 108, 120, 130) stitches evenly around armhole edge. Knit 5 rows. Bind off.
Sew side seams. Sew on buttons.

Chart for Back

└─4-st repeat─┘

Chart for Left Front

└─4-st repeat─┘

Chart for Right Front

└─4-st repeat─┘

Stitch key

☐ Knit on RS, purl on WS
▭ Knit on WS
☑ Sl 1 purlwise with yarn at WS of work

Color key

▨ MC
▨ CC

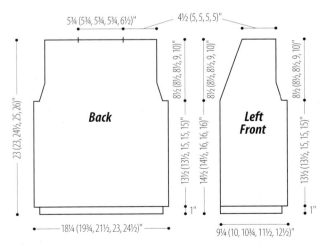

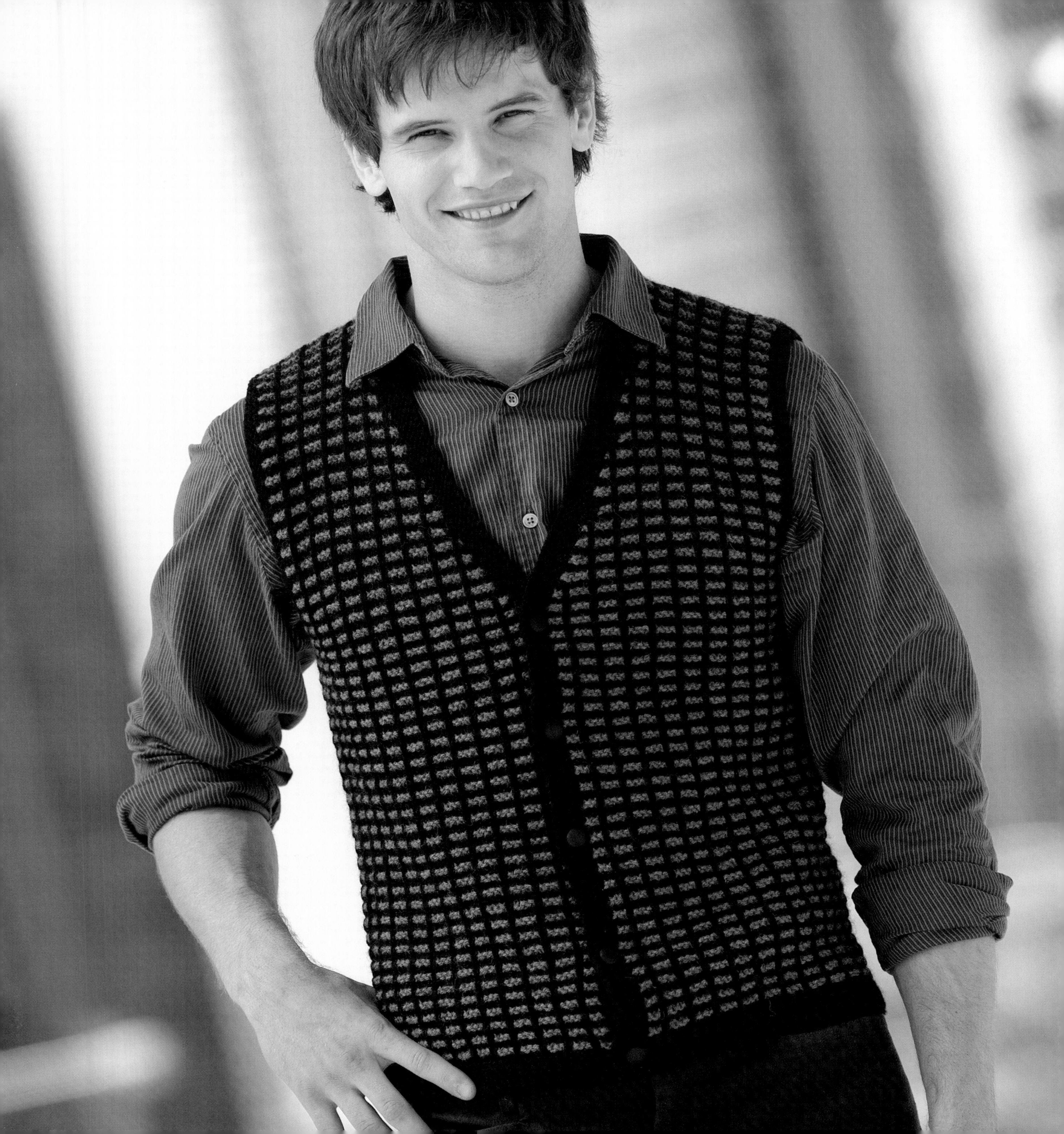

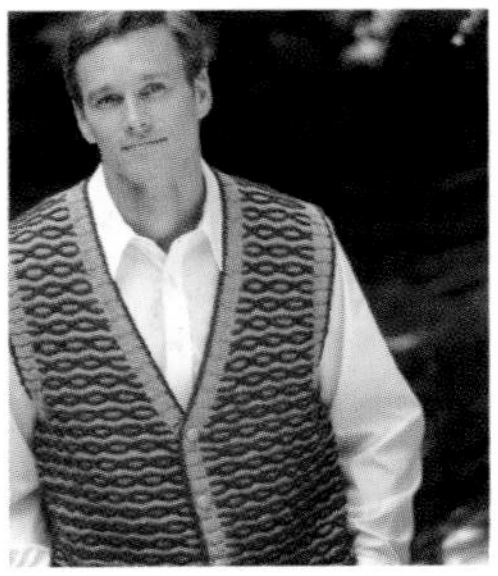

Relaxed comfort doesn't have to be plain or boring. The embossed chain design floats across the body of this man's cardigan in two unexpected colors.

Katharine Hunt

Embossed Chains

INTERMEDIATE

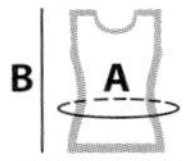
B
A

STANDARD FIT

Shown in Large
Sizes M (L, 1X, 2X)
A 44¼ (47¼, 50¼, 53¾)"
B 25½ (27¼, 28¼, 29)"

10cm/4"
38
21
• over Chart B, using larger needles

1 2 3 **4** 5 6
• Medium weight
MC • 650 (700, 800, 900) yds
A • 325 (375, 425, 500) yds
B • 250 (300, 350, 400) yds

• 3.75mm/US 5 and 4mm/US 6, or size to obtain gauge

• 3.75mm/US 5, 60cm/24" long

• 5 (5, 6, 6) 19mm/¾"

&
• cable needle (cn)
• stitch markers

original yarn
CLECKHEATON Country 8-ply Heathers (wool; 50g; 106 yds) Taupe (MC), Cranberry (A), and Earth (B)

Notes

1 See *School*, page 82, for 1-row buttonhole and cable cast-on. **2** When working decreases, do not work slip stitches at edge; work these stitches in stockinette stitch (knit on RS, purl on WS) instead.

Back

With smaller needles and A, cast on 142 (152, 162, 172) stitches. Work 9 rows of Chart A. ***Decrease row*** (WS) K2tog, * p3, k2tog; repeat from *—113 (121, 129, 137) stitches. Change to larger needles. Beginning and ending as indicated for back, work Chart B until 16 rows of chart have been worked 8 (8, 9, 9) times, then work first 8 rows of chart 0 (1, 0, 0) time more. Piece measures approximately 14¾ (15½, 16½, 16½)" from beginning.

Shape armholes

Bind off 11 (13, 13, 17) stitches at beginning of next 2 rows. Decrease 1 stitch each side on next row, then every other row 2 (4, 4, 4) times more, every 4th row twice—81 (81, 89, 89) stitches. Work even until armhole measures approximately 10 (11, 11, 11¾)" end with chart row 16 (16, 8, 16). Continue in stockinette stitch with MC only.

Shape shoulders

Bind off 8 stitches at beginning of next 2 rows, 7 (7, 8, 8) stitches at beginning of next 4 rows. Bind off remaining 37 (37, 41, 41) stitches.

Right Front

With smaller needles and A, cast on 72 (77, 82, 87) stitches. Work Chart A and Decrease row as for back—57 (61, 65, 69) stitches. Change to larger needles. Beginning and ending as indicated for right front, work Chart B until 16 rows of chart have been worked 7 (8, 8, 9) times, then work first 10 (2, 10, 2) rows once more. Piece measures approximately 14 (14¾, 15¾, 16½)" from beginning.

Shape V-neck and armhole

Decrease 1 stitch at neck edge (beginning of RS rows) on next row, then every other row 4 (4, 5, 5) times more, every 4th row 14 (14, 15, 15) times, AT SAME TIME, when piece measures same length as back to underarm, shape armhole at side edge only (beginning of a WS row and end of RS rows) as for back—22 (22, 24, 24) stitches. Work even until armhole measures same length as back to shoulder. Shape shoulder by binding off at beginning of WS rows 8 stitches 1 (1, 3, 3) times, 7 stitches 2 (2, 0, 0) times.

Left Front

Work as for right front, reversing shaping. Begin and end Chart B as indicated for left front. Shape V-neck at end of RS rows. Shape armhole and shoulder at beginning of RS rows.

Finishing

Block pieces. Sew shoulders.

Buttonband

With RS facing, circular needle, and MC, begin just above A row at lower edge of right front and pick up and knit 97 (102, 107, 112) stitches to beginning of V-neck shaping, 76 (81, 84, 84) stitches to shoulder, and 24 (24, 26, 26) stitches to center back neck—197 (207, 217, 222) stitches. Work rows 2–9 of Chart A. ***Next row*** (WS) * K2, p3; repeat from *, end k2. ***Next row*** With A, * p2, k3; repeat from *, end p2. Bind off in pattern on WS with A. With RS facing, smaller needles and A, pick up and knit 9 stitches along side of band at lower edge of right front. Bind off knitwise on WS. Join edges to form a continuous line of color. Place markers along band for 5 (5, 6, 6) buttons (each positioned in center of 3 knit stitches), with the first marker on the first k3 group at lower edge, the last at k3 group at beginning of V-neck shaping, and 3 (3, 4, 4) others spaced evenly between.

Buttonhole band

Work to correspond to buttonband, picking up stitches beginning at center back neck and ending just above A row at lower edge. Work 3-stitch, 1-row buttonholes over k3 groups on row 6 of Chart A to correspond to buttonband markers.

Armhole bands

With RS facing, smaller needles and MC, begin at underarm and pick up and knit 177 (197, 197, 217) stitches evenly around armhole edge. Work rows 2–9 of Chart A. ***Next row*** (WS) K2, p3, [k2tog, p3] 4 (5, 5, 5) times, * k2, p3; repeat from * to last 22 (27, 27, 27) stitches, [k2tog, p3] 4 (5, 5, 5) times, k2. ***Next row*** With A, knit the knit stitches and purl the purl stitches. Bind off in pattern on WS. Sew back neckband seam. Sew side seams. Sew on buttons.

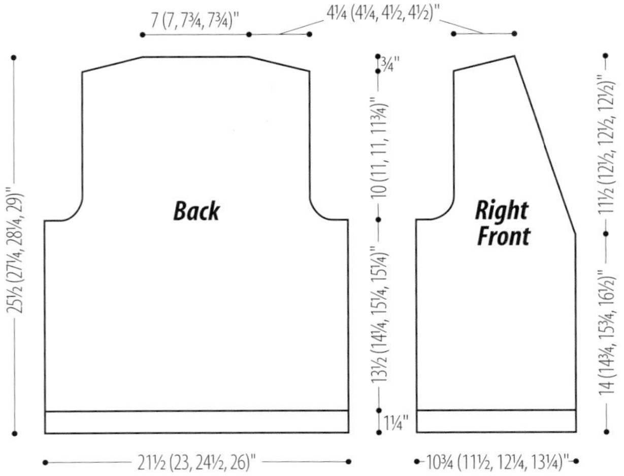
7 (7, 7¾, 7¾)"
4¼ (4¼, 4½, 4½)"
¾"
10 (11, 11, 11¾)"
13½ (14¼, 15¼, 15¼)"
1¼"
25½ (27¼, 28¼, 29)"
Back
Right Front
11½ (12½, 12½, 12½)"
14 (14¾, 15¾, 16½)"
21½ (23, 24½, 26)"
10¾ (11½, 12¼, 13¼)"

Chart A

9
8
7
6
5
4
3
2
1

←5-st repeat→

Chart B

16
15
14
13
12
11
10
9
8
7
6
5
4
3
2
1

←8-st repeat→

L Front
L, 2X

Back & L Front All
sizes; R Front M, 1X

R Front
L, 2X

Back & R Front All
sizes; L Front M, 1X

End

Begin

Color key

⬜ MC
🟦 A
🟪 B

Stitch key

⬜ Knit on RS, purl on WS

— Purl on RS, knit on WS

☑ Slip 1 purlwise with yarn at WS

▱ **1/2 RC** Sl 2 to cn, hold to back, k1; k2 from cn.

The whole is greater than the sum of its parts—and building it is easy! Striped triangles are worked in modular fashion to create a handsome vest for him.

Ginger Luters

Making The Grade

INTERMEDIATE +

LOOSE FIT

Shown in Extra Large (original) and Medium (reknit)

M (L, 1X)

A 46 (49, 52)"
B 23½ (24¼, 25)"

10cm/4"

36

18
• over Garter Ridge Pattern

1 2 **3** 4 5 6

• Light weight
MC • 415 (525, 575) yds
CC1 & CC3 • 125 (150, 175) yds each
CC2 • 350 (375, 400) yds
CC4 • 75 (100, 100) yds

• 4.5mm/US 7, or size to obtain gauge

• 4.5mm/US 7, 90cm/36" long

☺

• five 19mm/¾"

&

• stitch holder and markers

original yarn

RUSSI SALES HEIRLOOM
Heatherwood (wool; 50g; 105 yds)
Burgundy (MC), Medium Blue (CC1),
Rust (CC2), Light Blue (CC3), White (CC4)
Reknit (shown on pages 73 and 75)
JO SHARP Silkroad Aran Tweed (wool, silk,
cashmere; 50g; 104 yds) Russet (MC),
Licorice (CCI), Dusk (CC2), Ash (CC3), Twig (CC4)

Notes

1 See *School*, page 82, for SSK, S2KP2, lifted increase, short row wrap and turn (W&T), and 3-needle bind-off (ridge on RS). **2** Vest is worked in separate panels that are joined with 3-needle bind-off. **3** Count cast-on or pick-up row as first row of Garter Ridge Pattern. **4** Follow diagram to determine which CC to use in which triangle and for positioning of each triangle.

Garter Ridge Pattern

Rows 1 and 2 With MC, knit. *Row 3* (RS) With CC, knit. *Row 4* With CC, purl. Repeat Rows 1–4 for Garter Ridge Pattern.

Triangle A

Row 1 (RS) With MC, cast on 2 stitches. *Row 2* K2. *Row 3* With CC, k1, work lifted increase in next stitch (increase 1)—3 stitches. *Row 4* Purl. *Row 5* With MC, k2, increase 1—4 stitches. *Row 6* Knit. Continue in Garter Ridge Pattern, increasing 1 stitch at end of every RS row until there are 11 (12, 13) stitches, end with a WS row. *Next row* (RS) Knit to last 2 stitches, k2tog. Continue to decrease 1 stitch at end of every RS row until 2 stitches remain, end with a WS row. *Next row* (RS) K2tog. *Next row* P1. Fasten off.

Triangle B

Row 1 (RS) With MC, pick up and knit 22 (23, 24) stitches along edge of last triangle worked (see diagram). *Row 2* Knit. *Row 3* With CC, knit to last 3 stitches, k2tog, k1. *Row 4* Purl. *Row 5* With MC, repeat Row 3. *Row 6* Knit. Repeat Rows 3–6 until 2 stitches remain, end with a WS row. *Next row* (RS) K2tog. *Next row* P1. Fasten off.

Triangle C

Row 1 (RS) With MC, pick up and knit 22 (23, 24) stitches along edge of last triangle worked. *Row 2* Knit. *Row 3* With CC, k1, SSK, knit to end. *Row 4* Purl. *Row 5* With MC, repeat Row 3. *Row 6* Knit. Repeat Rows 3–6 until 2 stitches remain, end with a WS row. *Next row* (RS) SSK. *Next row* P1. Fasten off.

Triangle D

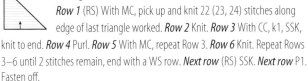

Row 1 (RS) With MC, pick up and knit 22 (23, 24) stitches along edge of last triangle worked. *Row 2* Knit. *Row 3* With CC, k1, SSK, knit to last 3 stitches, k2tog, k1. *Row 4* Purl. *Row 5* With MC, repeat Row 3. *Row 6* Knit. Repeat Rows 3–6 until 4 (5, 4) stitches remain, end with a WS row. *Next row* (RS) SSK, k0 (1, 0), k2tog. *Next row* K2 (k3, p2). *Next row* K2tog (S2KP2, k2tog). *Next row* P1. Fasten off.

Back

Work Panels 1-6.
Join Panels 1 and 2
(**Note** When picking up stitches along an edge, pick up 1 stitch for every garter ridge and 2 stitches for every stockinette stitch "valley" between ridges). With RS facing, CC2, and circular needle, pick up and knit stitches (as directed above) along right edge of Panel 2, ending at shoulder. *Row 1* (WS) Knit. *Row 2* With MC, knit. Set aside. With RS facing, CC2, and straight needles, pick up and knit stitches along left edge of Panel 1, ending at lower edge. *Row 1* (WS) Knit. *Row 2* With MC, knit. Then with WS together, join panels using 3-needle bind-off (ridge on RS) and MC, beginning at lower edge. When all stitches of Panel 1 have been used, bind off remaining stitches of Panel 2 purlwise. Join remaining panels of back in same manner. When joining Panels 5 and 6, bind off remaining stitches of Panel 5 knitwise.
Shape neck and shoulders
With RS facing and CC2, pick up and knit 56 (62, 68) stitches along top of back panels. Knit 3 rows. *Begin neck shaping: Next row* (RS) K22 (25, 27), bind off center 12 (12, 14) stitches, knit to end. *Next row* K22 (25, 27), place remaining stitches on hold. *Begin left neck and shoulder shaping: Row 1* (RS) Bind off 2 stitches (for neck), knit 16 (19, 21) more stitches, wrap next stitch (W&T) as follows: with yarn in back, slip stitch to right needle, bring yarn forward, return stitch to left needle, turn work. *Row 2 and all WS rows* Knit to end of row. *Row 3* Bind off 2 stitches, k12 (15, 16) more stitches, W&T. *Row 5* Bind off 2 stitches, k8 (11, 11) more stitches, W&T. *Row 7* Bind off 2 stitches, k4 (6, 6) more stitches, W&T. *Row 9* K14 (17, 19). *Row 11* K5 (7, 7), W&T. *Row 13* K7 (10, 10), W&T. *Row 15* K9 (12, 13), W&T. *Row 17* K11 (14, 16), W&T. *Rows 19-22* K14 (17, 19). Bind off.
Place stitches from holder onto needle, ready to work a WS row. *Begin right neck and shoulder shaping: Row 1* (WS) Bind off 2 stitches (for neck), knit to end. *Row 2 and all RS rows* Knit to end of row. *Row 3* Bind off 2 stitches, k14 (17, 19) more stitches, W&T. *Row 5* Bind off 2 stitches, k10 (13, 14) more stitches, W&T. *Row 7* Bind off 2 stitches, k6 (9, 9) more stitches, W&T. *Row 9* K5 (7, 7), W&T. *Row 11* K14 (17, 19). *Row 13* K5 (7, 7), W&T. *Row 15* K7 (10, 10), W&T. *Row 17* K9 (12, 13), W&T. *Row 19* K11 (14, 16), W&T. *Rows 21-23* K11 (14, 16). Bind off.

Left Front

Work Panels 7-9. Join panels as for back.

Right Front

Work Panels 10-12. Join panels.

Finishing

Sew bound-off stitches of front shoulder to tops of front Panels 8 and 11.

Armhole bands

With RS facing and CC2, pick up and knit 90 (96, 102) stitches evenly around armhole edge. *Row 1* (WS) Knit, working k3tog at each corner of underarm. *Row 2* Knit. *Row 3* Repeat Row 1. *Rows 4 and 5* With MC, repeat Rows 2 and 3. *Rows 6 and 7* With CC2, repeat Rows 2 and 3. Bind off. Sew side seams, being careful to match stripes in the triangles.

Lower band

With RS facing and CC2, pick up and knit 144 (156, 172) stitches evenly along lower edge. Work as for armhole band, omitting the decreases.

Front and neck band

Place markers for 5 buttonholes along left front edge, with the first ¾" below beginning of V-shaping, the last ½" above lower edge and 3 others spaced evenly between. With RS facing, circular needle, and CC2, pick up and knit 46 (48, 50) stitches along vertical edge of right front, 22 (23, 24) stitches along diagonal, 20 (21, 22) stitches along vertical edge of neck to tip of triangle, 38 (38, 40) stitches around neck, then pick up stitches down left front to match right front—214 (222, 232) stitches. *Rows 1, 3* and *5* (WS) Knit. *Row 2* Knit, working 3 decreases evenly spaced along back neck, 1 decrease at corners between Panels 8/9 and 11/12, and 1 increase at beginning of V-shaping on each front. *Row 4* With MC, knit, working 1 decrease between Panels 8/9 and 11/12, 1 increase at beginning of each front V-shaping, and working buttonholes at markers (by k2tog, yo). *Row 6* With CC2, repeat Row 4 (omitting buttonholes). *Row 7* Knit. Bind off.

Sew on buttons. Block lightly.

Color key
- ■ CC1
- ■ CC2
- ■ CC3
- ☐ CC4

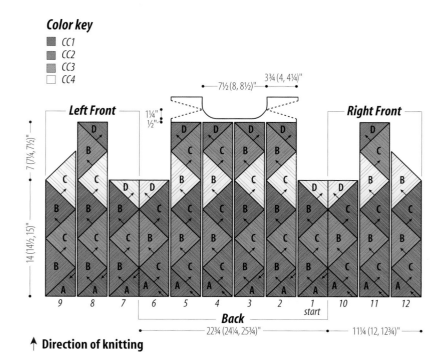

↑ Direction of knitting

Katharine Hunt

Zip out the cold in style! Katharine Hunt designed this crewneck cardigan vest in a great two-color pattern stitch for torso-warming style. Its slightly shorter length makes it comfortable for cool weather driving or horseback riding, and for layering under a parka.

Ripples and Cables

Note
See *School,* page 82, for zipper insertion.
Seed stitch *OVER AN ODD # OF STITCHES*
Row 1 * K1, p1; repeat from *, end k1. *Row 2* Knit the purl stitches and purl the knit stitches. Repeat Row 2 for Seed stitch.

Back
With 4.5mm/US 7 needles and A, cast on 101 (113, 129, 141) stitches. Work in Seed stitch for 4 rows. Change to 5mm/US 8 needles. Beginning and ending as indicated for back, work Chart Pattern until piece measures approximately 13¾ (14¼, 14¾, 15)" from beginning, end with chart row 4.
Shape armholes
Bind off 6 (8, 10, 10) stitches at beginning of next 2 rows. (*Note* If necessary, break B and reattach at appropriate point to work next row.) Decrease 1 stitch each side on next row, then every other row 3 (5, 3, 3) times, then every 4th row twice—77 (81, 97, 109) stitches. Work even until armhole measures approximately 8½ (8¾, 9¼, 9¾)", end with chart row 4.
Shape shoulders
Bind off 7 (8, 10, 11) stitches at beginning of next 4 rows, 7 (7, 10, 11) stitches at beginning of next 2 rows. Bind off remaining 35 (35, 37, 43) stitches.

Right Front
With 4.5mm/US 7 needles and A, cast on 45 (51, 59, 65) stitches. Work in Seed stitch for 4 rows. Change to 5mm/US 8 needles. Beginning and ending as indicated for right front, work Chart Pattern until piece measures same length as back to underarm, end with chart row 1. Shape armhole at side edge (beginning of WS row and end of RS rows) as for back—33 (35, 43, 49) stitches. Work even until armhole measures approximately 6 (6, 6½, 7)", end with chart row 2.
Shape neck
Next row (RS) Bind off 5 (6, 7, 8) stitches (neck edge), work to end. Decrease 1 stitch at neck edge every row 3 times, then every RS row 4 (3, 3, 5) times—21 (23, 30, 33) stitches. Work even until armhole measures same length as back to shoulder. Shape shoulder by binding off at beginning of every WS row 7 (8, 10, 11) stitches twice, 7 (7, 10, 11) stitches once.

Left Front
Work as for right front, reversing pattern and shaping. Begin and end Chart Pattern as indicated for left front. Shape armhole and shoulder at beginning of RS rows. Shape neck at beginning of WS rows and end of RS rows.

Finishing
Block pieces. Sew shoulders.
Neckband
With RS facing, 3.75mm/US 5 needles and A, begin at right front neck edge and pick up and knit 28 (30, 32, 34) stitches to shoulder, 35 (35, 37, 43) stitches along

back neck, and 28 (30, 32, 34) stitches along left front neck—91 (95, 101, 111) stitches. Work in k1, p1 rib for 2¾". Bind off in rib. Fold neckband in half to inside and sew in place along neckline.
Armhole bands
With RS facing, 3.75mm/US 5 needles and A, begin at underarm and pick up and knit 111 (121, 127, 137) stitches evenly around armhole edge. Work in Seed stitch for 3 rows. *Next row* (RS) Work 6 (8, 10, 10) stitches, [work 2 together, work 3 stitches in pattern] twice, work 2 together, work to last 22 stitches, work 2 together, [work 3 stitches, work 2 together] twice, work to end. Bind off in pattern.
Front bands
With RS facing, 3.75mm/US 5 needles and A, pick up and knit 115 (119, 127, 133) stitches along right front edge to top of neckband (picking up through both thicknesses of band). Work in Seed stitch for 4 rows. Bind off in pattern. Work left front band in same way. Insert zipper so that edges of front bands meet and conceal teeth. Sew side seams.

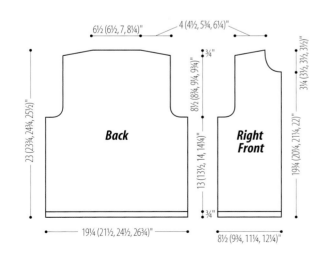

6½ (6½, 7, 8¼)"   4 (4½, 5¾, 6¼)"   ¾"   3¼ (3½, 3½, 3½)"

8½ (8¾, 9¼, 9¾)"

23 (23¾, 24¾, 25½)"   13 (13½, 14, 14¼)"

19¼ (20¼, 21¼, 22)"

Back   **Right Front**

¾"

19½ (21½, 24½, 26¾)"   8½ (9¾, 11¼, 12¼)"

Chart Pattern

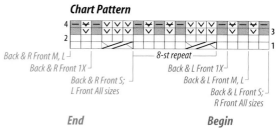

4
2
3
1

Back & R Front M, L
Back & R Front 1X
Back & R Front S;
L Front All sizes

8-st repeat

Back & L Front 1X
Back & L Front M, L
Back & L Front S;
R Front All sizes

End   **Begin**

Color key

☐ A
▨ B

Stitch key

☐ Knit on RS, purl on WS
— Knit on WS
☑ Slip 1 purlwise with
  yarn at WS of work
☒ Slip 1 purlwise with
  yarn at RS of work
⊠ *1/2 RC* Sl 2 to cn, hold
  to back, k1; k2 from cn.

Fit

Your measurements

Use pencil to note your measurements in the chart so that if you change size, the entries can be easily changed.

Across back ....
Shoulder to shoulder

Chest ....

Waist ....

Back length ....
Neck bone to hip

Hip ....

Wrist ....

Forearm ....
at fullest part

Upper arm ....
at fullest part

Center back ....
Length from wrist to center back;
arm should be slightly bent

Measure

Take measurements over a T-shirt or other close-fitting, lightweight garment.

Shoulder to shoulder (across back)
Locate the prominent bone where the arm joins the shoulder. Measure the distance between these two bones.

Chest
Measure around chest, keeping the tape measure parallel to the floor.

Waist
Measure around the waist.

Hips
Measure around the hips (6–8" below the waist). Before removing the tape, use another tape to measure the center back length from the base of the neck to the hip.

Arm
Take four measurements:
Around the wrist bone for a cuff
Around the forearm at fullest point
Around the upper arm at its fullest part
With arm relaxed at side of body, measure from the wrist bone around a slightly bent elbow to the shoulder and across to the center back. (This is the **C** measurement shown on each pattern's fit icon and is how sleeve length is measured for menswear.)

S

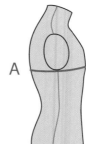
A

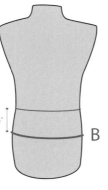
B

C

Men	Small	Medium	Large	1X	2X
Chest	34–36"	38–40"	42–44"	46–48"	50–52"
Center back (neck to cuff)	32–32½"	33–33½"	34–34½"	35–35½"	36–36½"
Back hip	25–25½"	26½–26¾"	27–27¼"	27½–27¾"	28–28½"
Cross back (shoulder to shoulder)	15½–16"	16½–17"	17½–18"	18–18½"	18½–19"
Sleeve length (to underarm)	18"	18½"	19½"	20"	20½"

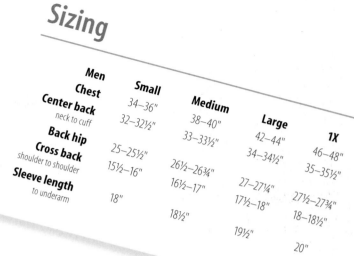

Compare

The **A**, **B**, **C** and shoulder width measurements (**S**) that determine the fit of a sweater are based on standards. But most of us are not a perfect size Large, or Small. Take our friend Roy. Although his chest measures 40", he is 45" at the waist and needs a Large sweater.

Measurement	Roy measures	Standard Large	The difference
A	45"	42–44"	Ease will take care of this
B	27"	27–27.25"	OK
C	34"	34–34.5"	OK
S	16"	17.5–18"	-1.5–2"

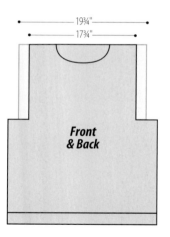

Front & Back

Proceed

Since Roy's shoulders are 2" narrower than the standard that our patterns are based on, we can refine the fit of his sweater by removing a few extra stitches (1") as we shape each armhole (front and back).

To maintain the sleeve length, we will add 1" (say 10 rows) to each of the sleeves.

In a similar way, you can shorten sleeves.

With this approach, you can turn most any drop-shoulder sweater into a modified drop-shoulder. Always consider any stitch or color pattern as you make these adjustments.

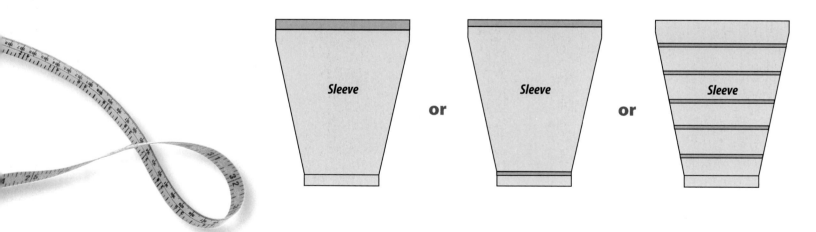

Sleeve   or   *Sleeve*   or   *Sleeve*

Color

Choosing color

It's hard to ignore color. The color of a sweater can make you love it or loathe it, be excited or bored by it. Here are other ways to color a few of our favorites.

Preview

With color wraps, crayons, or colored pencils, or Knitter's Paintbox you can create a colorway with very little effort.

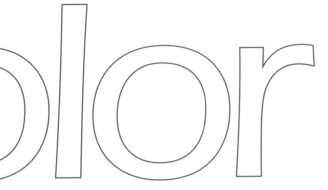

Knitter's Paintbox

Swatch

Swatch to get gauge and view the interaction of color within the knitting.

Positive or negative

Tweeds or solids

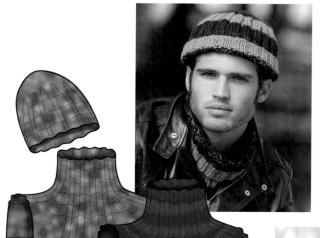

Work solids, stripes or let
the yarn do the work

Tone it down or Jazz it up

Place color strategically

Proceed

TECHNIQUES INDEX

3-NEEDLE BIND-OFF

Bind-off ridge on wrong side
1 With stitches on 2 needles, place **right sides together**. * Knit 2 stitches together (1 from front needle and 1 from back needle, as shown); repeat from * once more.
2 With left needle, pass first stitch on right needle over second stitch and off right needle.

3 Knit next 2 stitches together.
4 Repeat Steps 2 and 3, end by drawing yarn through last stitch.

Bind-off ridge on right side
Work as for ridge on wrong side, EXCEPT, with **wrong sides together**.

LONG-TAIL CAST-ON, KNIT

Make a slipknot for the initial stitch, at a distance from the end of the yarn, allowing about 1½" for each stitch to be cast on.
1 Bring yarn between fingers of left hand and wrap around little finger as shown.

2 Bring left thumb and index finger between strands, arranging so tail is on thumb side, ball strand on finger side. Open thumb and finger so strands form a diamond.

3 Bring needle down, forming a loop around thumb.
4 Bring needle **under** front strand of **thumb loop**…

5 …up **over index finger yarn**, catching it…

6 …and bringing it **under** the front of **thumb loop**.

7 Slip thumb out of its loop, and use thumb to adjust tension on the new stitch. One knit stitch cast on.

Repeat Steps 3–7 for each additional stitch.

CABLE CAST-ON

1–2 Start with a slipknot on left needle. Insert right needle into slipknot from front. Wrap yarn over right needle as if to knit. Bring yarn through slipknot, forming a loop on right needle.

3 Insert left needle in loop and slip loop off right needle. One additional stitch cast on.

4 Insert right needle **between** the last 2 stitches. From this position, knit a stitch and slip it to the left needle as in Step 3. Repeat Step 4 for each additional stitch.

CHAIN CAST-ON

A temporary cast-on
1 With crochet hook and waste yarn, loosely chain the number of stitches needed, plus a few extra chains. Cut yarn.
2 With needle and main yarn, pick up and knit 1 stitch into the back 'purl bump' of the first chain.

Continue, knitting 1 stitch into each chain until you have the required number of stitches. Do not work into remaining chains.

SSK

1 Slip 2 stitches *separately* to right needle as if to knit.

2 Slip left needle into these 2 stitches from left to right and knit them together: 2 stitches become 1.

The result is a left-slanting decrease.

S2KP2, sl 2-k1-p2sso

1 Slip 2 stitches *together* to right needle as if to knit.

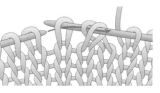

2 Knit next stitch.

3 Pass 2 slipped stitches over knit stitch and off right needle: 3 stitches become 1; the center stitch is on top.

The result is a centered double decrease.

S2KP2, sl 2-k1-p2sso ALTERNATIVE METHOD

1 Slip 2 stitches together to right needle as if to knit.

2 Slip next stitch to right needle as if to knit.

3 Knit these 3 stitches together by slipping left needle into them from left to right.

4 Completed: 3 stitches become 1; the center stitch is on top.

SSP

Use instead of p2tog-tbl to avoid twisting the stitches.

1 Slip 2 stitches *separately* to right needle as if to knit.

2 Slip these 2 stitches back onto left needle. Insert right needle through their 'back loops,' into the second stitch and then the first.

3 Purl them together: 2 stitches become 1.

The result is a left-slanting decrease.

SSK tbl

1 With yarn in back, slip 2 stitches, *one at a time*, purlwise through the back loop.

2 Slip both stitches back to left needle and knit these 2 stitches together.

Completed SSK tbl, a right-slanting twisted decrease.

K2TOG tbl

1 Knit next 2 stitches on left needle together through the back loops.

2 Completed k2tog tbl, a left-slanting twisted decrease.

MAKE 1 LEFT (M1L), KNIT

Insert left needle from front to back under strand between last stitch knitted and first stitch on left needle. Knit, twisting strand by working into loop at back of needle.

Completed M1L knit: a left-slanting increase.

MAKE 1 RIGHT (M1R), KNIT

Insert left needle from back to front under strand between last stitch knitted and first stitch on left needle. Knit, twisting the strand by working into loop at front of the needle.

Completed M1R knit: a right-slanting increase.

MAKE 1 LEFT (M1L), PURL

Insert left needle from front to back under strand between last stitch worked and first stitch on left needle. Purl, twisting strand by working into loop at back of needle from left to right.

Completed M1L purl: a left-slanting increase.

MAKE 1 RIGHT (M1R), PURL

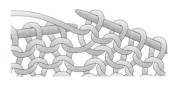

Work as for Make 1 Right, Knit, EXCEPT purl.

Completed M1R purl: a right-slanting increase.

INTARSIA - PICTURE KNITTING

Color worked in areas of stockinette fabric: each area is made with its own length of yarn. Twists made at each color change connect these areas.

TIPS
• Intarsia blocks are always worked back and forth, even in circular work.
• When bobbins are called for, make a **butterfly** or cut 3-yard lengths to prevent tangles.
• Work across a row and back before you untangle yarns.

Right-side row

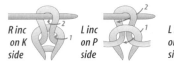
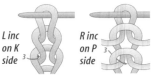

Wrong-side row

Making a twist:
Work across row to color change, pick up new color from under the old and work across to next color change.

LIFTED INCREASE, KNIT OR PURL

R inc on K side *L inc on P side*   *L inc on K side* *R inc on P side*

Work increase before stitch
Knit or purl into right loop of stitch in row below next stitch on left needle (1), then knit or purl into stitch on needle (2).

Work increase after stitch
Knit or purl next stitch on left needle, then knit or purl into left loop of stitch in row below this stitch (3).

1-ROW BUTTONHOLE

1 (Right-side row) Bring yarn to front and **slip 1 purlwise.** Take yarn to back and leave it there. * Slip next stitch, then pass previously slipped stitch over it; repeat from * for each buttonhole stitch. Put last slipped stitch back onto left needle.
2 Turn work. Bring the yarn to back and **cable cast on** as follows: * Insert

right needle between first and second stitches on left needle, wrap yarn as if to knit, pull loop through and place it on left needle; repeat from * until you have cast on 1 stitch more than was bound off.
3 Turn work. Bring yarn to back, slip first stitch from left needle, pass extra cast-on stitch over it, and tighten.

Note
In Step 2, try leaving yarn in front and cable cast-on as if to purl. The result is shown in the photo below.

3-ROW BUTTONHOLE

Row 1 (Right-side) **SSK, yarn over** twice (as shown).
Row 2 Purl into first yarn-over, drop second off needle.

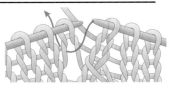

Row 3 Knit into yarn-over space in row below. Pull stitch off left needle and let it drop.

USING STEEKS

1 A V-neck vest:
The shaded areas are the steek stitches; x's are the decreases for shaping the armhole and neck.

2 Secure both edges of each steek (at front and armholes) with crochet or machine-stitching (see instructions below).

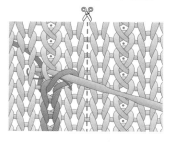

3 Cut steeks to make openings.

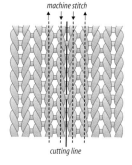

4 Work bands, neaten inside edges, and wear.

CROCHET-AND-CUT STEEK

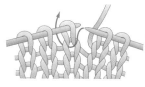

1 Prepare for the crochet steek by knitting the stitch before and after the center steek stitch ***through the back loop***.
2 Holding yarn on the wrong side and crochet hook on the right side, chain through each twisted stitch. Work a chain stitch in every round from bottom to top.
3 Cut through the center of the steek to form an opening. Continue with Step 4, above.

STITCH-AND-CUT STEEK

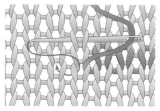

With contrasting yarn, mark center of steek by basting down center stitch. Make 2 parallel rows of stitching on each side of the basting yarn (stitch down the right or left leg of the stitches, not between the stitches). Cut through center stitch following basting yarn. Continue with Step 4, above.

CROCHET CHAIN STITCH (ch st, ch)

1 Make a slipknot to begin.
2 Catch yarn and draw through loop on hook.

First chain made. Repeat Step 2.

DUPLICATE STITCH

Duplicate stitch (also known as **swiss darning**) is just that: with a blunt tapestry needle threaded with a length of yarn of a contrasting color, cover a knitted stitch with an embroidered stitch of the same shape.

KNIT 1 ROW BELOW (k1b)

1 Instead of working into next stitch on left needle, work into stitch directly below it.

2 Pull stitch off left needle and let it drop.

ZIPPERS

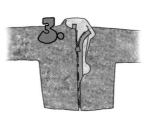

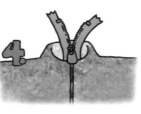

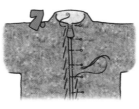

Sewing a zipper into a knit requires care. Although the knitted fabric has stretch, the zipper does not, and the two must be joined as neatly as possible to prevent ripples. Here are the steps to follow for a smooth zipper placement:

1 Measure the length of the opening. Select a zipper that matches the length of the opening or is a bit longer.
2 Pre-shrink your zipper by washing it as you will wash the garment.

3 Lay the garment flat, making sure that the sides match up.

4 If you are using a zipper that is too long, align at bottom, allowing extra to extend beyond neck.

5 Pin the zipper in place. Be generous with the pins; extra care taken here makes the next steps easier.

6 Fold under any extra fabric at the top of the zipper and secure with pins.

7 Baste the zipper in place. When you are satisfied with the placement, remove the pins.

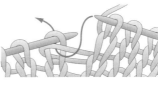

8 Sew in the zipper, making neat, even stitches.

9 If the zipper extends beyond the opening, trim extra length.

10 Reinforce stress points at the top and bottom edges.

GRAFT IN GARTER

ON THE NEEDLES

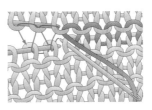

1 Arrange stitches on 2 needles so stitches on lower, or front, needle come out of purl bumps and stitches on the upper, or back, needle come out of smooth knits.
2 Thread a blunt needle with matching yarn (approximately 1" per stitch).
3 Working from right to left, begin with Steps 3a and 3b:
3a Front needle: bring yarn through first stitch *as if to purl,* leave stitch *on needle.*
3b Back needle: repeat Step 3a.
4a Front needle: bring yarn through first stitch *as if to knit, slip off* needle; through next stitch *as if to purl, leave on* needle.

4b Back needle: repeat Step 4a. Repeat Steps 4a and 4b until 1 stitch remains on each needle.
5a Front needle: bring yarn through stitch *as if to knit,* slip *off needle.*
5b Back needle: repeat Step 5a.
6 Adjust tension to match rest of knitting.

SHORT ROWS / WRAP & TURN (W&T)

STOCKINETTE STITCH

Each short row adds 2 rows of knitting across a section of the work. Since the work is turned before completing a row, stitches must be wrapped at the turn to prevent holes. Wrap and turn as follows:

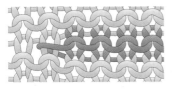

Knit side
1 With yarn in back, slip next stitch as if to purl. Bring yarn to front of work and slip stitch back to left needle (as shown). Turn work.
2 With yarn in front, slip next stitch as if to purl. Work to end.

3 When you come to the wrap on a following knit row, hide the wrap by knitting it together with the stitch it wraps.

GARTER STITCH

1 Slip stitch purlwise with yarn in back. Bring yarn to front and slip stitch back to LH needle. Turn work and knit next row.

Purl side
1 With yarn in front, slip next stitch as if to purl. Bring yarn to back of work and slip stitch back to left needle (as shown). Turn work.
2 With yarn in back, slip next stitch as if to purl. Work to end.

3 When you come to the wrap on a following purl row, hide the wrap by purling it together with the stitch it wraps.

Purl a purl wrap
The first stitch of each short row is slipped (Step 2); this tapers the ends of short rows. When the wraps are hidden (Step 3), the mechanics of the shaping are almost invisible.

2 Short row with wrapped stitch.

BEGINNER BASICS

KNIT CAST-ON

 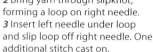

1 Start with a slipknot on left needle (first cast-on stitch). Insert right needle into slipknot from front. Wrap yarn over right needle as if to knit.

2 Bring yarn through slipknot, forming a loop on right needle.
3 Insert left needle under loop and slip loop off right needle. One additional stitch cast on.

4 Insert right needle into the last stitch on left needle as if to knit. Knit a stitch and transfer it to the left needle as in Step 3. Repeat Step 4 for each additional stitch.

KNIT

1 With yarn in back of work, insert right needle into stitch on left needle from front to back.

2 Bring yarn between needles and over right needle.

3 Bring yarn through stitch with right needle. Pull stitch off left needle.

4 Knit stitch completed.

PURL

1 With yarn in front of work, insert right needle into stitch from back to front.

2 Bring yarn over right needle from front to back.

3 Bring yarn through stitch with right needle. Pull stitch off left needle. Repeat Steps 1–3.

BIND OFF KNITWISE

1 Knit 2 stitches as usual.
2 With left needle, pass first stitch on right needle over second stitch (above) and off needle: 1 stitch bound off . (next drawing).

3 Knit 1 more stitch.
4 Pass first stitch over second. Repeat Steps 3–4.
When last loop is on right needle, break yarn and pull tail of yarn through loop to fasten (see Fasten off).

BIND OFF PURLWISE

Work Steps 1–4 of Bind-off Knitwise **except**, purl the stitches instead of knitting them.

FASTEN OFF

Work bind-off until only 1 stitch remains on right needle. If this is the last stitch of a row, cut yarn and fasten off stitch as shown above. Otherwise, this is the first stitch of the next section of knitting.

WORKING FROM CHARTS

Charts are graphs or grids of squares that represent the right side of knitted fabric. They illustrate every stitch and the relationship between the rows of stitches.
Squares contain knitting symbols.
The key defines each symbol as an operation to make a stitch or stitches.
The pattern provides any special instructions for using the chart(s) or the key.
The numbers along the sides of charts indicate the rows. A number on the right

side marks a right-side row that is worked leftward from the number. A number on the left marks a wrong-side row that is worked rightward. Since many stitches are worked differently on wrong-side rows, the key will indicate that. If the pattern is worked circularly, all rows are right-side rows and worked from right to left.
Bold lines within the graph represent repeats. These set off a group of stitches that are repeated across a row. You begin

at the edge of a row or where the pattern indicates for the required size, work across to the second line, then repeat the stitches between the repeat lines as many times as directed, and finish the row.
The sizes of a garment are often labeled with beginning and ending marks on the chart. This avoids having to chart each size separately.

ABBREVIATIONS

CC contrasting color

cn cable needle

cm centimeter(s)

dpn double-pointed needle(s)

g gram(s) "inch(es)

inc increas(e)(ed)(es)(ing)

k knit(ting)(s)(ted)

M1 Make one stitch (increase)

m meter(s)

mm millimeter(s)

MC main color

oz ounce(s)

p purl(ed)(ing)(s) or page

pm place marker

psso pass slipped stitch(es) over

RS right side(s)

sc single crochet

sl slip(ped)(ping)

SKP slip, knit, psso

SSK slip, slip, knit these 2 sts tog

SSP slip, slip, purl these 2 sts tog

st(s) stitch(es)

St st stockinette stitch

tbl through back of loop(s)

WS wrong side(s)

wyib with yarn in back

wyif with yarn in front

yd(s) yard(s)

Yo yarn over

specifications:

Pattern Specifications

Skill level

INTERMEDIATE

STANDARD FIT

Fit
Includes ease (additional width) built into pattern.

Sizing

Sizes XS (S, M, L, 1X, 2X)
Shown in Small
A 35½ (38½, 41½, 47½, 53½, 56½)"
B 20½ (21½, 23½, 25, 26, 27)"
C 27 (28, 28½, 29½, 31, 31½)"

Garment measurements
at the A, B, and C lines on the fit icon

10cm/4"
32
24
• over Chart pattern using larger needles

Gauge
The number of stitches and rows you need in 10 cm or 4", worked as specified.

1 2 **3** 4 5 6

Yarn weight
and amount in yards

• Light weight
• 1498 (1605, 1819, 2140, 2568, 2889) yds

Type of needles
Straight, unless circular or double-pointed are recommended.

•3.75mm/US5 and 4.5mm/US7, *or size to obtain gauge,* 60cm/24" long

☺

Buttons

•7 (7, 8, 8, 9, 9) 25mm/1"

&

Any extras

•stitch holders
•stitch markers

Yarn information

original yarn

RUSSI SALES Heirloom Easy Care 8
(wool; 50g; 107 yds)

Measuring

• **A** Chest
• **B** Body length
• **C** Center back to cuff (arm slightly bent)

Fit

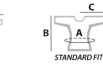
CLOSE FIT
chest plus 1–2"

STANDARD FIT
chest plus 2–4"

LOOSE FIT
chest plus 4–6"

OVERSIZED FIT
chest plus 6" or more

Sizing

Measure around the fullest part of your chest to find your size.

Men	Small	Medium	Large	1X	2X	3X
Actual chest	34–36"	38–40"	42–44"	46–48"	50–52"	54-56"

at a glance

Conversion chart

centimeters		0.394		inches
grams		0.035		ounces
inches	X	2.54	=	centimeters
ounces		28.6		grams
meters		1.1		yards
yards		.91		meters

Needles/Hooks

US	MM	HOOK
0	2	A
1	2.25	B
2	2.75	C
3	3.25	D
4	3.5	E
5	3.75	F
6	4	G
7	4.5	7
8	5	H
9	5.5	I
10	6	J
10½	6.5	K
11	8	L
13	9	M
15	10	N
17	12.75	

Equivalent weights

¾	oz	20 g
1	oz	28 g
1½	oz	= 40 g
1¾	oz	50 g
2	oz	60 g
3½	oz	100 g

Yarn weight categories

Yarn Weight					
1	**2**	**3**	**4**	**5**	**6**
Super Fine	**Fine**	**Light**	**Medium**	**Bulky**	**Super Bulky**

Also called

Super Fine	Fine	Light	Medium	Bulky	Super Bulky
Sock Fingering Baby	Sport Baby	DK Light-Worsted	Worsted Afghan Aran	Chunky Craft Rug	Bulky Roving

Stockinette Stitch Gauge Range 10cm/4 inches

27 sts to 32 sts	23 sts to 26 sts	21 sts to 24 sts	16 sts to 20 sts	12 sts to 15 sts	6 sts to 11 sts

Recommended needle (metric)

2.25 mm to 3.25 mm	3.25 mm to 3.75 mm	3.75 mm to 4.5 mm	4.5 mm to 5.5 mm	5.5 mm to 8 mm	8 mm and larger

Recommended needle (US)

1 to 3	3 to 5	5 to 7	7 to 9	9 to 11	11 and larger

Yarn substitutions

Throughout this book, the photo caption describes the yarns and colors in the photograph. If a yarn is not available, its yardage and content information will help in making a substitution. Locate the Yarn Weight and Stockinette Stitch Gauge Range over 10cm to 4" on the chart. Compare that range with the information on the yarn label to find an appropriate yarn. These are guidelines only for commonly used gauges and needle sizes in specific yarn categories.

Contributors

Oscar *Britt*

Kathy *Cheifetz*

Linda *Cyr*

Susan *Z. Douglas*

Georgina *Estefania*

Norah *Gaughan*

Julie *Gaddy*

Katharine *Hunt*

Elsebeth *Lavold*

Heather *Lodinsky*

Ginger *Luters*

Nancy *Marchant*

Uschi *Nolte*

Elaine *Rowley*

Barbara *Venishnick*

Lois *Young*

Diane *Zangl*

Kathy *Zimmerman*